Flowers and Promises
A True Story

By Hanna Vanora

ISBN 978-1-105-19025-4
ID 11768260

Table of Contents

Author's Preface

In writing this book, I would like to relate the pattern of domestic abuse and its affect on my own life and others around me. Maybe you know someone that's in a similar situation or you yourself are in this type of situation.

Not too long ago, while my family was up on the mountain camping, my sister-in-law told me that she and some of my other family members had sat and discussed my possible funeral, where I would be buried, who would take care of my kids, etc. I could have easily ended up dead in the relationship I was in. When she first told me this, it had little effect on me. I was desensitized and detached. I've had time to heal and engage in a healthy relationship since then, so when she reminded me of it, I was stunned and it made much more of an impact on me! I felt inspired with an overwhelming need to share my experiences and to reach out to others that may be going through similar circumstances.

As you read this true story, look for the following characteristics listed on the next few pages, the unhealthy patterns in my relationships, and how my thought perceptions kept me in it for so long.

The end of this book contains useful information on how to get help for yourself or someone you know, and how to create a safety plan.

There *is* a way out and there *is* hope!

*Names have been changed.

Cycle of Violence

Phase I: Rising Tension Phase

Man: Increasingly irritable, frustrated, feels he is losing control.

Woman: Frightened, tries extra hard, withdraws, may precipitate incident to diffuse tension. There is a feeling of 'walking on eggshells'.

Phase II: Acute Battering Incident

The tension explodes in a physically and/or emotionally abusive incident. The victim is most often blamed for the incident and may blame herself.

Phase III: Honeymoon Phase

Man: Contrite, loving, tender, courting behavior, promises reform.

Woman: Loving, forgiving, believes man wants to change.

The abuser says he is sorry, begs for forgiveness, and promises it won't happen again and may say that he will get counseling. Physical intimacy is often coerced. The seriousness of the incident is minimized.

Phase IV: Cycle Starts Again.

The next time the assault occurs, chances are it will be more severe. Statistics indicate that the abuse becomes more severe over time.

Types of Abuse:

- Pushing, shoving, kicking, hitting, slaps, choking, pinching, shaking, hair pulling, spitting on you, etc.
- Keeps you from leaving
- Holds you down
- Destroys objects/throws objects at you
- Abandons you, possibly in dangerous places
- Subjects you to reckless driving
- Refuses to help you when you are ill, injured, or pregnant
- Threatens or uses weapons against you
- Abuses or kills pets to hurt you
- Destroys or sells your possessions
- Calls you names
- Forces sex/stripping against your will
- Minimizes your feelings about sex
- Accuses you of flirting or having affairs
- Publicly shows interest in others
- Has affairs after agreeing not to
- Commits sadistic sexual acts
- Criticizes, humiliates, ridicules you
- Ignores your feelings
- Shouts or screams at you
- Keeps you from working or jeopardizes your job
- Controls all money or takes away money (economic abuse), makes all decisions
- Threatens to hurt you or your family
- Manipulates with lies and contradictions
- Refuses to work
- Isolates you from family and friends
- Threatens to kidnap or harm children or use the children against you
- Uses intimidation

These methods of emotional abuse and brainwashing have been used on prisoners of war before. Does any of this sound familiar to you?

Isolation:

Abuser uses threats, demands, and manipulation to cut victim off from other people. Victim becomes dependent on abuser for everything, including social contact.

Monopolizing Attention:

Victim feels she needs abuser's approval for everything. Victim 'walks on eggshells' to keep abuser from getting angry. Abuser resents and tries to get rid of anything that competes for victim's attention.

Inducing Exhaustion Weakness:

Victim is physically injured, deprived of sleep, or constantly in fear. Begins to feel she is completely helpless and cannot take any action for her self.

Threats:

Abuser keeps victim in constant fear and anxiety by making threats to harm her or the things she loves, or to leave her, ruin her reputation, or embarrass her.

Occasional Indulgences:

Abuser gives victim gifts or tokens of affection to keep her hoping for more, usually right when he realizes he's gone too far and she's about to leave.

Demonstrating Omnipotence:

Abuser claims to be all-powerful and always right, and does things to demonstrate this, and to demonstrate how weak and stupid the victim is.

Degradation:

Abuser ridicules victim, or ignores her, or forces her to do degrading things or actions she believes is wrong.

Enforcing Trivial Demands:

Abuser insists things be done his way, forces victim to do small things for him that he could do himself, criticizes what victim does, forces her to account for all her time.

Crazy-making:

Abuser denies or lies about reality so much that victim begins to doubt herself. Abuser makes good qualities seem bad, makes false accusations, and tells victim she's crazy or stupid.

Dynamics of the Batterer

- Low self-esteem
- Is a traditionalist
- Believes the stereotyped masculine sex role of dominance and expects the female to be passive
- Blames others for his actions or problems
- Has hypersensitivity; is easily hurt or offended
- Is pathologically jealous; abuser says it is a 'sign of love'
- Dr. Jekyll and Mr. Hyde personality; one minute he is nice and the next he is exploding
- Uses sex as an act of aggression; uses 'playful' use of force in sex
- Does not believe his behavior should have negative consequences
- Experiences most emotions as anger
- Socially isolated; few friends
- Uses isolation to cut the other person off from all resources, family, and friends
- Quick involvement; is married, engaged, or living together within six months of getting new partner
- Minimizes and denies seriousness of violence
- Abuses alcohol and/or drugs
- Witnessed abuse as a child or was abused as a child
- He 'really loves her and needs her' and has unrealistic expectations; expects partner to meet all of his needs
- Has a need to be in control but has very little self-control
- Tends to over-compensate in an effort to take charge
- Controlling behavior; batterer will say he is concerned for the other's safety
- Is cruel to animals or children
- Verbally abusive; degrades other person, curses the other, runs down anything the other accomplishes
- Has past history of abuse
- Uses threats of violence to control the other person

- Breaks or strikes other objects to terrorize the other person into submission
- Uses any force during an argument; may involve holding a woman down, physically restraining her from leaving the room, or any pushing or shoving

Common Beliefs Held by the Batterer about Their Victims:

1. Women are manipulative. *Allows batterer to feel like the victim.*
   a. Women lie, cheat, and steal to provoke men. They started it. They get what they deserve.
   b. Women say 'no' when they mean 'yes'. *This discounts the victim's feelings.*
2. Women think of men as a paycheck. *This allows the batterer to feel used.*
3. If I don't control her, she will control me. *Batterer feels like the victim.*
   a. If I don't strike back, she'll henpeck me for life. *Abuse is self-protection.*
4. Women want to be dominated by a strong man. *Batterer discounts the victim's feelings.*
5. I have the right to choose my partner's friends. *Control is self-protection.*
6. I can't change unless my partner changes too. *Excusing lack of change.*
   a. My partner is half the problem. *Blaming partner.*

Dynamics of the Victim

- Low self-esteem or sense of inferiority
- Learned helplessness
- Is a traditionalist
- Believes in myths
- Wants family unity
- Believes the stereotyped feminine sex role of inferiority and passiveness
- Accepts responsibility for her batterer's actions
- Is in denial
- Perceives abuser as all-powerful and unstoppable
- Believes that she has a good man with problems she can help him solve
- Minimizes and denies the danger
- Suffers from guilt but denies the terror and anger she feels
- Has the strength to manipulate her environment, sometimes to prevent further violence
- Is passive with the abuser, yet strong in other areas
- Is isolated
- Has severe stress reactions with psycho psychological complaints
- Uses sex to establish intimacy
- Believes that no one will be able to help her resolve the predicament except herself
- Economically and emotionally dependent on spouse or lover
- Accepts violence as normal behavior
- Searches for a solution
- Tries to reduce batterer's displeasure
- Fails to leave

- *Packet from Utah Workforce Services*

Though it might seem inconceivable that a battered woman would keep returning to the person causing her pain, the pattern is utterly typical. Studies have shown that two-thirds of battered women who leave their abusers go back within a year or two; it takes the average survivor five tries before she escapes for good. "Leaving this kind of relationship is a process, because of the huge influence the abuser has on the victim," says Veronique Valliere, Psy.D., a clinical psychologist in Fogelsville, PA, who specializes in treating abuse victims and perpetrators. "She can't just pick up and leave; the abuser makes that impossible by the control he exerts over her life." There's only one way most women can get out of this kind of relationship, says Sheryl Cates, the former CEO of the Texas Council on Family Violence, and that's with outside help. "I would say the vast majority of women who leave do it only with the support of family or friends," Cates asserts.

Domestic Abuse Stories - Battered Woman Escapes Domestic Abuse - Good Housekeeping

Prologue

How had I gotten myself to this dreadful place? Hadn't I learned anything from my past experience? I just seemed to keep getting myself drawn further into this horrifying relationship. How quickly I would forget why I had made my previous escape from him. I always thought I was doing the right thing by going back.

I had a large black garbage bag full of our most-needed things ready and waiting next to the back door. We were already in the process of moving, so the garbage bag was not conspicuous. I was so scared that he would catch me trying to leave. What then? What would he do to me? I surely didn't want to find out! In the times I had left before, I had gotten away safely enough. I feared the worst if he awoke during my getaway this time, even though in the past he had always been deeply sorry for how he had acted. He always managed to convince me to come back with pleading, tears, flowers, and promises. I would then feel as if I had gained some power over the situation. I thought I could handle it better the next time. I got stronger and more confident when I was away from him. Unfortunately, each time I went back, it was only to be torn down worse than the time before. My life depended on *this* escape.

I felt such an immense amount of guilt for what my kids had gone through, what *I* had put them through by staying in the situation, because of my naivety, low self-esteem, and insecurities. If only I had paid attention to the warning signs in the beginning...

Chapter 1

My Childhood

When I was young, I loved going to visit my mother. She was beautiful and fun and most importantly, I felt her genuine acceptance of me. My parents were divorced and my dad had custody of the four of us; me, my older sister, and my two brothers - one older and one younger. I only saw my mom on Thanksgiving and Easter one year, and then Christmas the next, in addition to two months during each summer. That was our visitation agreement. I remember being so sad without her. Soft Musk and spearmint gum were the scents I missed most about her. I asked her to give me her perfume bottle so I could smell it whenever I needed to feel her near. I counted the days until I would be able to see her again, which always felt like an eternity. I had a wonderful stepmom though, and that helped ease the pain. My dad married her when I was four years old. She hadn't been married before and didn't have any children. She had a degree in teaching and taught home economics. She was a wonderful seamstress and she made most of our clothes. I felt genuine acceptance from her also, which was really good for my self value. It was important to me that I felt worthy of someone's attention. She taught me and my siblings so many things and always tried to help us discover our talents. She praised us often, taught us songs and games, took us to church, read to us, and took a million pictures. I'm surprised we weren't blinded from the flash on the camera! She always had fun, creative ideas and things for us to do to keep us occupied. I'm sure it was quite challenging for her to take on four children all at once.

I don't remember much of my life up until that point in time, only bits and pieces. I remember being left unattended quite often. My older brother and I got into many things we weren't supposed to. We were in the basement a lot and broke the large glass jars of peanut butter that lined the shelf, along with other items of food storage, and rather enjoyed sticking our fingers in it and licking them clean. Luckily, we never got any glass in our mouths. I remember watching my sister come down the stairs following a stream of smoke once because my older brother had started a fire in the basement. Even without my brother near, I still managed to get into all kinds of things I shouldn't have; I painted my mom's bedroom door with acrylic paints (I was confused about why the tubes had a 'pin' in the top and so I tried to pull them out first), I started the bath water and let it run until it overflowed, I climbed on the counters and got into the cookies, I threw eggs at our house and the passing cars with my neighbor, and I poured out the sugar canister onto the floor. My sister told me once that she felt so bad because our babysitter had paid her to keep quiet about leaving me and my brothers in the basement for quite some time while they left and went to town. She remembered it being light outside when they left, and dark when they returned. She missed a lot of school from staying home and helping take care of us. It was a hard time for her, and her teacher was not kind about it. She was only eight years old, five years older than me. Many mornings, upon my waking, I remember feeling helpless and not being able to find my way around the house because my eyes were sealed shut with infection. I would feel my way up to the top of the stairs and then wait for my sister to find me and clean my eyes off with a warm washcloth. I know my mom had to work a lot in order to pay the bills. I don't remember her at home often, and apparently our babysitter was not reliable.

A good memory I do have from that time was while sitting on my mom's bed with her and her new husband and her teaching me how to sing the 'Jack and Jill' nursery rhyme. I thought my new stepdad was mean because he teased a lot and he looked big and scary to me. I did like that he and my mom owned a pet store. I loved to play with the turtles that roamed around freely throughout the store. I was delighted to slowly follow them around. I had to watch my hands near them because they liked to snap. There were a lot of big tanks that held a wide variety of fish. I remember being so fascinated with the tiny little sharks, the quarter-sized turtles, and the extra-large snails that clung to the sides of the tanks. My stepdad once brought home a King snake, two love birds, and some fish. I found them to be quite amusing, especially the snake. I wasn't afraid of it in the least and held it whenever I had the opportunity. I guess I was a bit of a tomboy in some ways and wished I could be a boy like my big brother. I refused to wear a shirt when I could get away with it, which was usually only when we went to the lake and I got to wear my cut-off jeans and nothing more.

My mom seemed happy with this man and he treated her kindly as far as I knew. However, later on in life, he became the second largest coke dealer in Utah and spent time in prison for planning a hit on a federal agent. Nice, huh? Although I missed my mother terribly, it seems at the time it was probably a good thing we went to live with our dad.

My dad worked as an electrician up until he had a heart attack when I was ten years old. He had to have a triple bypass surgery and was on disability from then on. My stepmom utilized her teaching degree and went back to work as a school counselor to support our family. She was well-liked in our community and did her job exceptionally well. We didn't have a lot of money, so we spent most of our vacations camping in the mountains. We loved camping and fishing and sitting around the fire at night roasting marshmallows, sometimes just to watch the flames engulf them. My dad would teach us where to get dry firewood and how to build a fire. He taught us how to fish too, but I was much too impatient to sit and wait and often reeled in the line hoping I had a bite. After a while, I would stop fishing and go look for snakes. I gave my dad a bit of a scare once because I was bitten by a snake I had picked up and he didn't know what kind it was. Thankfully it was only a Blow snake. After that day, I didn't pick them up anymore unless I knew what kind they were and if they were safe.

My dad kept the house immaculate, cooked a hot breakfast for us each morning (we considered cold cereal to be a treat), did the laundry, and took care of the yard. We had the biggest and most beautiful weed-free vegetable garden in the neighborhood. He helped us get our homework done and made sure our grades were up. He also worked part time for a while at a juvenile detention facility. On his softer side, he was always helping the elderly in our neighborhood. He would chop wood and do yard work for them and take them his homemade bread.

He made wheat bread each week. I think my parents put wheat in everything they cooked because it was 'good for us'. It was always a delight to come home to the wonderful scent of fresh-baked bread with melting butter on top, especially after a long day at school. I loved it when my dad was happy. He was really silly when he was in a good mood. He would dance funny dances and say things to make us all laugh. He could be quite the comedian. We knew when it was time to be serious though, as he was rather strict in our daily routines and scripture study. I didn't like reading scriptures. I found it hard to stay awake. I've never been much of a morning person and scripture study was at 6 a.m. at the kitchen table, which we all knew better than to be a minute late for! My little brother and I would play silent games across the table from each other by trying to see if we could get the other to crack a smile. At least it was entertaining and kept me awake.

We have always been a close family. We had our normal sibling rivalry of course, but we were still the best of friends. We didn't really have a choice; we spent most of our playtime and activities together. I didn't have other friends over often. I was always embarrassed and thought my parents were weird. I didn't realize at the time that a lot of other kids thought the same thing of their parents too. I also felt self-conscious about looking poor. We had a nice enough house; it was just a regular normal-sized home. It was out in the country about five miles from town. It was beautiful out where we lived with the mountains in the not too far distance and the smaller hills close enough we could walk to them. We would drag our inner tubes (these made great sleds and flotation devices) up the hill during the winter and slide down the snowy slopes. Afterwards, we would trudge back home to warm up by the wood burning stove downstairs, sip on a steaming mug of hot chocolate, and munch on cinnamon toast. In the spring, we'd ride our bikes or horses up there just to explore and enjoy the warm weather.

We were clean and simple. I really had no reason to be embarrassed but I just felt different from others. I hated our family car; it really *was* embarrassing. It was a Ford Galaxy 500 and I figured it must be at least a hundred years old. It was turquoise colored with 'rust highlights'. Once, when I was a bit older, I bought my parents a window sticker to put in it that read, 'rust is my favorite color'. I was in the process of learning that it's much easier to laugh at the things you can't change. In spite of my unreasonable insecurities, I just preferred going over to my friend's houses instead, although it seemed it was always a hassle to do so. We had to plan it two weeks ahead of time and have it written on our calendar. Yes, my parents were planners. I'm sure I drove my dad crazy because I was spontaneous and carefree and enjoyed taking my time with everything I did. I hated planning, and honestly, what friend was going to want to plan a sleepover two weeks ahead of time? Needless to say, I spent a lot of time at home and filled it by playing outside or reading books in my bedroom. Reading seemed to help me feel like I could escape my 'boring life' and live the ones I read about for the moment. I was grateful to my stepmom for taking us to the library so often.

My mother was different than my dad. He was more of the authoritarian type of parent, and she was more of the permissive type. I loved the freedom that came with my time at her house. I rode my bike all over town, went swimming at the public pool with friends, went to movies, had sleepovers at my cousin's house, bought candy, explored, flirted with boys, watched what I wanted on television, played night games with the neighbor kids, drank a lot of hot chocolate at the local café, and spent a lot of time at the reservoir swimming, skiing, and sun-tanning. I could wear the clothes I wanted to, which I wasn't allowed at my dad's. I thought it was good to be modest, but I considered him to be ridiculous and overboard in his idea of modesty. I know he was trying to be protective, but I didn't understand that back then. I thought he just wanted to ruin my teenage life and make me as miserable as possible.

With this freedom, I managed to stay out of trouble for the most part. It helped that my mom lived in a small town where almost everyone knew each other. If they didn't know you, it was certain they knew your parents or grandparents, or some other relative. It felt safe. I never heard police sirens; in fact, the only time I ever saw a cop was when I was at the café having hot chocolate and they were sitting at the counter enjoying a cup of coffee and visiting with the locals.

My mother married her 3rd husband, Ray, when I was ten years old. She had two children with him, my little sister and littlest brother. He was always nice to me and I liked him. I could usually tell if someone genuinely liked me or if they were a fake, and he seemed genuine. I thought he was quite fun. He would even let me drive his truck sometimes and was always laughing and joking around. My mom was happy. She and my aunt taught us cooking, tole-painting, needlework, and sewing in 4-H during the summers I was there. I received blue ribbons with everything and I was proud of my accomplishments.

My mom was only married to him for a couple of years and then they divorced. I remember one night when he came to the house drunk and had a gun in hand. He wanted to shoot my mom's new boyfriend. Too bad he didn't. He was holding my little sister in one arm and had the gun in the other. I remember looking up at him and asking him to please not do this. He stopped. Later that night, me, my mom, and my older sister went to the movies. I guess that was a way to help ease the tension and stress from the events that had taken place earlier that evening, and it worked.

My mom's 4th husband, the boyfriend that almost got shot, was a nice enough guy, too nice at times. He loved to fish and cooked a lot of breaded perch for us. I thought it was really good! I hated him after I found out he had thrown a living room chair at my mom and broke her arm. I hated him even more after they got divorced and my young sister informed me about what he had done to her when she was three years old. I had to write it all down so my mom could submit it in court. My heart ached for my dear little sister. He had molested her. Apparently nothing happened to him however, and he got away with it. He went on to marry again and had a daughter of his own, who he also molested and got away with.

One day, he came over to our house after all this had come out about my sister. I walked out of my bedroom to see him standing in the kitchen talking to my mom. I, in a very snotty voice, asked him what *he* was doing there. I didn't wait for his reply. I glared at him and went back into my room. I was fourteen at the time and had gone to live with my mom. I came out a little later to see if he was gone. He was, and so were my little sister and brother. I asked my mom where they were and she said they were with him. He'd taken them with him to go for a ride to the dump. I couldn't believe it! I was absolutely dumbfounded! How on earth could she have allowed that? She said 'he just missed the kids'. I was so angry with her! I didn't understand. How could she possibly let him in our house, and even worse, allow the kids to be left alone with him?

Chapter 2
High School Years

As a teenager, I had become quite angry with my dad and had grown hateful of him and my stepmom. I felt picked on and didn't feel like he liked me. I didn't like my stepmom anymore simply because she was not my real mother. I felt trapped and desperately wanted the freedom I had when I was at my mom's. I finally convinced my dad to let me go live with her. I know this upset him greatly, but I didn't care. I just wanted what I thought would be my ideal life. I went to live with her right before I turned fourteen and before starting the 9th grade, which was part of high school in the small town I was moving to. She wasn't married at the time but had gotten a new boyfriend. My mom was really having a hard time. I babysat my younger brother and sister when I wasn't at school, sometimes overnight. I got a little resentful about it at times, but I didn't mind too much for the most part. I felt like 'the mom'. I wanted to join some of the school activities or sports but I didn't feel like I had the support I needed, and for some reason, I felt a little intimidated about joining anything. I really just needed a good push in the right direction, some encouragement, and someone to believe in me and my abilities. I was athletic, loved dancing, and had a lot of potential. However, I didn't know where to start and didn't realize that had I joined some of those school activities, I might have had some common ground with more of the other girls. Maybe then I wouldn't have felt so lonely.

One night my mom's boyfriend was at our house and he had a little pill bottle he was trying to hide. I didn't know what was in it but he told me not to tell anyone about it, as if I knew what it was. That's just great, I thought, another winner. He was just another dumb guy that I wasn't about to let my guard down to or allow myself to get close to. Besides, he'd probably be gone soon, as that seemed to be the ongoing pattern. I tried to be nice to him anyway, for my mom's sake.

My mom was taking medication, although I didn't know what it was for. He told me not to let her take more than one. I tried really hard to watch her and make sure she did only take one. She let me know she was okay and told me not to worry about it and that she was going to bed. She tried to commit suicide that night. She was taken to the hospital and her boyfriend came back and yelled at me for not watching her. What an idiot! I was hurting for my mom and he had the nerve to try to make me feel like it was my fault! I felt really bad, but I refused to accept that kind of responsibility. Why did my mom keep choosing people that were not good? I just wanted her to be happy. As it turned out, he was married and had a son, both things he had forgotten to mention to my mom. He went back to them once he'd been found out. Good riddance.

At the end of my 9th grade year in school, still age fourteen, I remember sitting in class when I was called to the office. I left the room and headed down the hall. On my way there, I saw my Aunt Marie and my mom's friend walking toward me. I knew something was wrong. I asked them, yet they wouldn't tell me. I kept asking who it was about and went through a list of family members that might be in trouble or harmed in some way and tried to get them to tell me what was going on. Finally, when we got out to the car, they informed me that my little brother, who was three years old at the time, had fallen into a fast-flowing irrigation ditch and had been flown to Salt Lake City to the children's hospital. My mom had been looking at a house to buy earlier that day and all the kids had been playing outside. One of them came in and said my brother had fallen into the water. An ambulance was called and the Search and Rescue team came to help. My uncle was a member of the Search and Rescue team and he was the one to find and pull my brother out of the water. They estimated that he had been under water for about thirteen minutes. My aunt drove me to the hospital where my brother was and we met my mom there. It was so surreal to see him lying there in the bed, lifeless, with tubes and wires all over him. He was in a coma.

My mom spent much of her time at the hospital before my brother was transferred to a nursing home. She stayed in Salt Lake and went to see him there each day until the end of the summer, then she moved back home. She brought him home to visit whenever she was able to. I lived with my aunts for the remainder of the school year and throughout most of the summer while my mom was away. One of my aunts that I stayed with, who was my mom's sister, lived in a duplex with her children. Tyler was a year older than me, and Holly was a year younger. I liked being at their house, but I felt like my aunt didn't think too highly of me. I know she cared about me, but I got the impression that she considered me to be some kind of bad girl, which I wasn't. She always assumed I was going to meet up with some boy or something. I just wasn't like that, but I couldn't seem to convince her otherwise.

I was close to my cousins. We had a lot of fun hanging out together. One night, I stayed up late watching television with Tyler. I was lying on the couch and he sat at the end of it. I was getting pretty tired, as it was near 1 a.m. I fell asleep with my feet on his lap but awoke in a petrified terror. He was touching me under my shorts! I froze. I couldn't believe it! I moved around as if I was waking up and he told me to go back to sleep. I was in total shock. He started up again, so I sat up suddenly and asked him *why* he would do that to me! I went outside and sat on the porch to process what had just happened. He came out and sat next to me. I didn't know what to say or what to do, but I was really mad! I let my mom know about it the next time she was in town. She said she would talk to my aunt. I asked my mom later what was said and I was told that my aunt would 'talk to Tyler about it'. After their talk, according to my aunt and Tyler, it was basically 'my fault because I was lying on the couch with shorts on and my feet on his lap'. I guess they figured I was 'just asking for it'. Nothing happened to Tyler and I felt like I was viewed as a slut. I then felt it was necessary to prove I was *not*. I couldn't just 'not worry about it' like my mom had advised me. I felt really self-conscious about it for a long time. I went to church on my own sometimes, I tried changing friends to ones that were looked upon as really good kids, I tried to act extra-religious, and I felt I simply could not be myself.

When my mom moved back from Salt Lake, we went to live with my grandpa, who was an active alcoholic at the time. He did overcome it years later and got clean and sober through the help of family and AA, but he was really struggling with my grandmother's death back then. She had passed away a few years earlier from cirrhosis of the liver. She had also been an alcoholic. It was interesting and sad to see what alcohol could do to a person. He drank from the time he got up until the time he went to bed. He never seemed to really be 'with it'. I would catch him 'talking' to my grandmother across the kitchen table late at night. I really felt sorry for him. It was so sad to see him that way. My mom had also been through a lot for quite some time, and I felt like I was on my own. I was depressed and lonely. I suffered from insomnia and it took me several hours to fall asleep each night. Needless to say, it was really difficult to get up and go to school. I was late and unprepared more often than not and my grades were falling. I felt unsocial and like everyone viewed me as a bad girl. I seldom smiled and people were always telling me I needed to 'smile more'. It wasn't as easy as it should have been.

There was a boy at school that I really liked and wanted to have as my boyfriend. I had had a crush on him for the previous year and a half. I desperately wanted someone to just care about me and take away my loneliness. I thought he was so cool and extremely good looking, so I tried to be around him whenever I could. One night, a cousin of mine and the guy I really liked came and picked me up and we went driving around. They were drinking and offered some to me. I wanted to impress this guy and didn't think it was such a big deal. After a while, my cousin dropped us off at some seemingly deserted camp trailer in the middle of nowhere. I don't remember it all very well because the alcohol had taken an effect on my thinking. He moved really fast. It wasn't something I had planned on and it just seemed to happen so quickly. I didn't know the first thing about what I was supposed to do. All I knew was that I couldn't say no to him. It didn't matter that I wasn't ready. It didn't matter that I didn't know anything about sex. Needless to say, it was not the most pleasant experience for me.

I was so scared the next day. I couldn't believe what I had done. I was afraid. What if I was pregnant? As it turns out, I was not pregnant, but I had to worry for a while since I didn't understand how everything worked. I was only fifteen and had limited knowledge on the subject.

We went together for a month after that. We held hands as we walked down the halls at school and hung out in our free time. I called him each day and we would sit on the phone for about an hour talking about nothing. I thought that was the thing to do when you're 'going out'. I started feeling self-conscious though, and it was difficult to just be myself around him. Consequently, he had his friend call me one day out of the blue to tell me he wanted to break up. I went in the bathroom and sat in the bathtub crying my eyes out. I felt such rejection. I felt like I must not have been good enough for him. The next day at school, I saw him holding hands with his ex-girlfriend and walking her to class. It was more than I could bear. I just wanted to be far away from that town and that school!

My life felt dark and empty. I was struggling to keep my head above water and I knew I needed help. The only thing that really made me happy was my dog. I loved my dog! I brought him home one day without asking, just hoping that I would get to keep him. My mom had a soft heart and let me have him. He was half German Shepherd and half Brittney Spaniel. I had always wanted a German Shepherd; I considered them to be the prettiest and most awesome breed of dogs. He was good for me. I had the responsibility of taking care of him and training him, which gave me purpose. He was always happy to see me and kept me company.

Aside from playing with my dog, I spent much of my time after school riding my grandpa's horses in the field next to his house or on the three-wheeler. As the cold weather began, I developed a pretty bad cough and got pneumonia. My immune system wasn't functioning well, which was probably due to a lack of sleep. I didn't quite know how to ask my mom for help - mostly because I didn't know what it was that I needed, and she had been struggling so much that I didn't want to bother her. She had a new boyfriend; he was ten years younger than her. He seemed okay, but rather needy. All I cared about was that my mom was happy. If he made her happy, then I wasn't worrying about her as much. Anyway, I believed the solution to my problems would be to go back to my dad's house and live there for a few months, just long enough to get back on my feet and get my grades up. My mom was so mad at me when I asked her if I could go back to my dad's. For some time, she wouldn't look at me or talk to me hardly at all. I imagine she must have felt pretty hurt, but I went anyway; I felt it was best for me.

After I got to my dad's, I eventually realized he had no intention of letting me go back to my mom's again. I was devastated. My grades did go up, but I was still depressed. I felt like my dad hated the sight of me. He didn't like my dog and let me know it all the time. He had to be tied up outside and I didn't spend as much time with him because I had to wear 'outside clothes only' just to go out and pet him. I don't know exactly what happened with my relationship with my dad. It seemed to change when I became a teenager. I wasn't happy, and he wasn't happy, which didn't make a good combination. I fought him on everything, but he always won, and I felt helpless and trapped. I hated feeling controlled and I considered him to be a controlling father. I wasn't doing so well socially at school. I seemed to struggle with that a lot and it was quite lonesome. I had acquaintances and people liked me all right, but having friends to hang out with and have fun with outside of school was difficult for me because I didn't feel like I could just be myself. I was unhappy and felt insecure. I didn't know what the solution was and I didn't know how to change it.

One day, my dad and I were having a discussion in the kitchen. I don't remember how it started or what we were talking about, but I do remember asking him why he had such a hard time with me. He told me I reminded him of my mother. I do look a lot like her. We both have blonde hair and brown eyes. I have a lot of her features - high cheek bones, similar noses, same height, slim build, and similar mannerisms. In a few sentences later, he told me he hated her. I took that rather personal. It was as if he had just told me I reminded him of my mom, who he hated, so much that he couldn't stand me either. At that moment, I got pretty angry. I even yelled at my dad; something I had never done before! I didn't care what happened. I wanted him to know how upset that made me! I turned around and punched a hole in the wall, then crumpled to the floor in a heap and started crying. He picked me up and held me for a long time. I know he loved me, but our personalities just seemed to clash. He fixed the hole in the wall without a word.

Finally, my dad agreed to let me go live with my Aunt Marie. She lived in the same town as my mom, so I would still get to see my mom often. However, my dad absolutely refused to let me live with my mom when she had a boyfriend living with her who she was not married to. My mom thought my dad did things like that to control her. I think it was wise to not have me live there, despite the reasons between them. The 'needy' boyfriend of hers hit her in the head one day and the doctor said if it had been 1/4" higher, it would have killed her. She had suffered brain cancer a few years earlier and had to have surgery twice to remove it. She was in a dangerous position to be receiving any kind of trauma to her head. He didn't live with her anymore after that.

I did extremely well at my Aunt Marie's house. I started taking an anti-depressant just before I moved there. They built a bedroom for me and fixed it up nicely. I felt at home and I knew I was welcome there. I practically lived there during the summers anyway because my cousin, Josie, was also my best friend. Growing up, we had more sleepovers than nights without them it seemed. We were always together.

I worked at the USU extension office during the summer before starting 11th grade and then got a job at the pizza place when school started, so I had a little extra money to do what I wanted with. I opened a bank account and learned how to manage my checkbook. I joined clubs at school, I was outgoing and social, I got good grades, and I felt happy! That was the best time of high school for me. Things were finally looking up. I didn't think the anti-depressants were doing anything for me, so I stopped taking them.

I went to stay with my mom for a few days during the winter and got to go out with my cousin, Holly, for a little while one night. We'd been invited to a party that was being held at one of the motels in town. We went, but after a short time, Holly was ready to leave. There had been a guy there that was flirting with me a lot and he asked me to *please* come back to the party after I took my cousin home. I was a little reluctant, but did it anyway. Once I had returned, they offered me some alcohol, which I drank a little of. I had to use the bathroom and when I was getting ready to come back out, he pushed me back in and turned off the light. He started kissing me and being rather pushy. I pushed him away from me and let him know I needed to leave. He asked if he could walk me out to my vehicle, which I allowed him to do. Once we were out there, he wanted to know if he could just sit and talk with me for a few minutes. I let him in my vehicle to talk. That quickly changed to him kissing me again and trying to do more. I kept telling him I needed to go and he needed to stop, but he didn't. Unfortunately I didn't *physically* try to enforce my words to get him off me. I went along with it even though I was telling him I didn't want to do what he was wanting. I don't know why I let him intimidate me that way. After a few minutes passed, I told him I *really* needed to go home and was able to convince him to get out of my vehicle. I stayed home from school for the entire week afterwards and cried all day, every day. I felt so guilty and *bad*. I saw him again the following week at the grocery store. He was with his girlfriend who he'd said he'd broken up with. He totally ignored me.

I don't know exactly when I started to feel depressed again, but life started to seem quite dreary. I often contemplated driving off the road into the drain each time I passed it. It was a steep canal without any water in it. I just felt sad and didn't know why. I did miss my mom and wanted to go live with her again. I spent my time at her house whenever I could. Her boyfriend didn't live there anymore, so I convinced my dad to let me go live with her. I was doing so well at my aunt's, yet I longed to be with my mom. I knew I would have more freedom than I had at my aunt's, but of course being a teen, more freedom was always most attractive. I did realize that if I wanted to graduate high school, I would have to do it because *I* wanted to - nobody else was going to make me do it or stay on top of it for me. I was in charge of myself.

I was on the Yearbook Staff at school and sometimes traveled out of town to take photos of different sporting events. This time, I was headed to a college to take photos of the wrestling tournament. One of my friends wanted me to meet her brother who was attending school there. She found him at the tournament and introduced us. His name was Aaron. He was nineteen, which was three years older than me, but that didn't seem like a big deal. He had been drinking and wanted to go get some food, so he asked if we wanted to go with him and if I would drive his car. It was an awesome 1969 black Camaro. Needless to say, I felt rather special. We all laughed and had a good time and headed back to the college. My friend said he seemed quite interested in me, which we giggled about, and then went about watching the rest of the event.

My mom met a new guy toward the end of my junior year. He was really smart and quite humorous. He seemed different than some of the men she had previously dated. He was stable, responsible, clean-cut, and overall he was a likeable man. The only thing I didn't like was that my mom suddenly started acting different. I believe she wanted to impress him and thought being stricter with me was the way to do it. Ugh! I was sixteen years old and had been doing just fine the way things were, so this was most annoying, but kind of comical at the same time. He became her 5th husband and I got a new stepsister and stepbrother.

Sometime at the end of June, I was home alone when the phone rang. It was my little sister's dad, Ray. He asked if my sister was there, then if my mom was there. Neither of them were home, so he started talking to me instead. At some point in the conversation, he said he had something important to tell me but that he had to wait until I was eighteen. I asked him if it had something to do with my dad. You see, I had had my doubts over the last couple of years about him being my real father. I didn't look like him. I even checked my birth certificate to see if he had signed it as my father. Only my mom's signature was there. I looked through my mom's old yearbooks searching for any man that could possibly resemble me. It was as if some part of me knew, but I chose to believe I was just being silly imagining there was any truth to the matter.

As soon as I asked if it had anything to do with my dad, I was stunned that the question had even come out of my mouth. Why would I ask him that? He was silent for a moment. He slowly said 'yes' and I felt a shock. I asked, "Does it have anything to do with him *not* being my dad?" Again, he was silent for a moment and then replied 'yes' a second time; another wave of shock. I warily formed the words in my mouth and asked, "Do you know who my dad is?" He slowly replied with a 'yeah'.

There was a silent moment and then he said, "Ray is your daddy." I was taken aback. I was in shock and trying to register all of this new information. I guess my silence made him wonder what I was thinking and he asked if it was okay that he was my dad. I laughed and told him that it was okay. It really *was*; I just couldn't believe how betrayed I felt. I don't remember anything else that was said after that. The rest was just a blur.

After I hung up the phone, I sat for a moment and wondered how I was supposed to act around my mom now. I was angry and hurt. I had been lied to my whole life up to that point. How many people knew? Should I tell her I know? Was that why my dad didn't seem to like me? Was that why I felt acceptance from Ray while he was married to my mom years ago? Why didn't he want to be my dad? I had so many questions whirling in my brain. I was recently grounded and wasn't supposed to leave the house, but I grabbed the keys and left anyway. I didn't care. I drove around for a while and then went out to my Aunt Marie's. I let her know what had happened and cried on her shoulder. I asked her if she knew about it, and yes, she did. I couldn't understand how they all could keep this from me!

I drove back to town and as I turned a corner, I saw my mom in her car, and she saw me. I glared at her and kept driving. I knew she would be mad at me for leaving the house when I had been grounded, but I just kept going. She waved at me to pull over, but I refused and kept driving. She continued to follow me, so I took her on a little goose chase, driving faster and turning all the corners trying to lose her. I took some pleasure in knowing how mad I must be making her. I didn't care. I thought she deserved it. I *wanted* her to be mad! After I lost her, I headed back home. I was ready to face her if I had to.

As she walked through the front door, she yelled at me to give her the keys and then shouted, "How can I trust you?"

I screamed right back at her, "How can I trust *YOU*?" That kind of stopped her in her tracks and she looked puzzled and a bit shocked that I would yell at her like that. I had never spoken that way to her before.

"What is *that* supposed to mean?" she asked curtly.

I headed toward my bedroom and screamed, "Who is my dad?" I knew then that she would figure out what had brought this unusual kind of behavior out of me. I didn't wait for her reply. I went in my room and slammed the door. She was right behind me and tried to open my door. I shouted at her to leave me alone and held the door shut. I screamed at her and told her I hated her. Finally, she gave up and left me alone to cool down.

I was still quite upset the next day, but I called my dad to tell him the news. When I let him know I knew he wasn't my biological father, his reply was simply, "I'm still your father and nothing changes that for me. I love you very much and you are my daughter." I don't know what kind of reaction I expected from him, but it wasn't that. Sometimes he surprised me with his calm yet firm affirmation on things.

Chapter 3
Aaron

The next night, I went out with my cousins, Holly and Josie. They were trying to cheer me up with a girl's night out. We sat parked on Main Street watching as the cars passed by. That was something all the high school kids did for fun. It was like an open invitation to have people pull over to hang out with you. Holly was friends with Aaron's little sister and she let me know that Aaron was home from college and had been asking about me. Well that was kind of exciting and flattering to me, and as we were talking about it, he drove by in his truck. We decided to follow him around for a bit. We followed him to the swimming pool, where Holly said he had been a life guard before moving away to college. We decided that we needed some candy and the swimming pool was a great place to go get it. Yes, that would be our excuse for being there. As we walked in, he stopped talking to the girl he was standing next to and watched me as I made my way to the counter. We quickly got our candy, laughing and giggling, and then left. He watched me as we walked out the door. I was thrilled to have caught his attention like that. We headed back to Main Street to 'drag main' as everyone called it. Dragging main was when you drove up and down Main Street repeatedly. It seems silly now, but when you were in high school, that was also a lot of fun. As we were dragging main, he drove up beside us and asked us to pull over. I got pretty nervous at that point. I never knew quite how to act around a guy I was interested in. We pulled over and started chatting. I kept pretty quiet mostly and felt sort of shy, so my cousin Josie did most of the talking. She was great at flirting. He finally asked me if I wanted to go see a movie with him. I was really excited, but I was so nervous that I was sweating. I thought Aaron was popular and outgoing, both of which I was not; at least I didn't think so. I was attracted to that, and I loved all the attention he was giving me.

On our first date, we went to see an Indiana Jones movie. After the movie, he grabbed my hand on our way out of the theater. I don't know why I was so nervous, but I think I hid it pretty well. I sat next to him in his truck and we drove around talking for a while, then he took me home. I went out with him each night after that. It was July and there was plenty of playing to do on the warm summer nights. Fireworks, parties, and just hanging out were all on the agenda. Sometimes we had to go check the water on his family's crops. While we were out there one night, he taught me how to do the Western swing dance and then we gazed at the stars while he pointed out different constellations to me. I was falling for this guy quickly. After the first week, my mom grounded me for being out too late. I think she figured it was getting serious and needed to put on the brakes a bit. I thought she was just being a little absurd.

In August, Aaron invited me to go with him and his dad to their family ranch in Colorado. They had a cabin there on several acres of land. I begged my mom to let me go and she finally gave in, as long as his dad was going too. It was so beautiful there. We rode horses all day and watched the lightening storms at night. I thought Aaron's dad was the nicest old man around. Aaron told me that his dad was a heavy drinker and that nobody really enjoyed being around him as they were growing up. He wasn't that way so much anymore. He was sweet and treated me well.

September rolled around and Aaron invited me to his family's ranch again; this time he was going with his friend Will, and Will's girlfriend Brandi. My mom wouldn't let me go no matter how much I begged. I felt crushed. It wouldn't be long until he had to go back to college and I wouldn't get to see him much anymore.

Upon Aaron's return, it slowly came out that he had gone with Will, Brandi, and Brandi's little sister, Ally. That stung. He promised me he wasn't 'with' her, they were just friends. However, after talking a while, it turns out they slept in the same room, then that changed to them sleeping in the same bed, yet 'nothing happened between them'. I wanted to believe him, and I put all my trust in him. If he said that's the way it was, then I would accept it as true.

Fall came and he went back to school. He lived in Salt Lake in an apartment with Will. I went to visit him a couple of times and sometimes he came back to our hometown to see me. He was pretty upset when he came to my house once, and said that he and his dad had gotten into a fight. He said his dad tried to take his keys and that he'd accidentally run over him because his dad was hanging onto the side of the truck as Aaron drove off. It only injured his dad's knee and they kept that whole incident quiet from his mom. I couldn't imagine having a fight like that with one of my parents! I didn't think Aaron was respectful to his parents.

I was having a bad day one time and decided I would skip school, get the money out of my checking account, and head to Salt Lake to surprise Aaron. I really did surprise him, and he didn't like it. He asked me not to do that again. Their apartment was obviously a place where they held parties from time to time. They always had alcohol and stories to laugh about. We sat and talked in his room for a while when I noticed earrings on his nightstand and then later found a pair of panties stuck in his bed, so I questioned him as to whom they belonged to. He told me right away they belonged to Brandi. Brandi had a small son and he said she was lying down by him to get him to sleep, and his room was a quiet place; also, her and Will had slept in there once. I believed him, reluctantly, but I couldn't imagine that he would do such a thing to hurt me. Boy, was I naïve.

One of the times Aaron was back visiting our hometown, we sat parked in a grocery store parking lot on Main Street when my stepsister and my older sister pulled up next to us. I was sitting beside him in his truck when they walked up to the window. My stepsister was friends with Ally, Brandi's little sister. She asked Aaron why he was getting his pants out of Ally's car the night before. He looked like he'd just seen a ghost. He had some excuse, although I don't remember what he said. My sisters accused him of cheating on me and advised me to dump him, and then they left. He started crying and begged me not to dump him and said that it had honestly just been a misunderstanding. I believed him, but I started feeling uneasy about our relationship.

One of my good friends was Will's younger sister, Kristen. She was dating one of Aaron and Will's friends, Sheldon, so she often went to Salt Lake to see him. She was a senior in high school like me, so we made a plan to graduate early and move to Salt Lake where we would start college and get an apartment together. I remember her trying to talk me out of going to Salt Lake to surprise Aaron that time I was having a bad day. I thought that was a bit weird, but brushed it off quickly. She knew. Everybody knew, except me. I guess I was blinded by my desire or need to have that relationship.

I got pregnant that October. I was on the verge of deciding to break up with Aaron, but I changed my mind when I found out I was going to have his baby. He often talked of wanting to have a baby; I just didn't think it would happen that soon. My mom had asked me in the previous month if I needed to get birth control, but I was mortified and bashfully told her no, as though I would never do such a thing.

I worked hard to finish school early, as I had planned to do anyway. Aaron asked me to marry him by getting down on his knee with a bouquet of red roses in hand and a beautiful diamond ring tied into them. We planned our wedding for the following January. Aaron was home from college during the Christmas vacation break, so we were able to spend a lot of time together then.

On New Year's Eve, we went to a party together where I found him flirting with another girl. I walked out of the kitchen to see her sitting on his lap. I was so angry! I went over and informed him that what he was doing wasn't okay with me and he needed to stop. Somehow during the party, I lost track of him and came to find out he had left the party with this girl. I was outraged! I asked my friends, Kristen and Sheldon, to please take me to find him. We went driving up and down Main Street for a while when finally we saw him driving back to the party with her. He had been drinking a lot. He always drove drunk; he believed he was a better driver drunk than sober and thought I was unreasonable by trying to convince him otherwise. Back at the party, I took him into another room and basically lectured him while he lay there drunk. I asked him how he could do this only two weeks away from our wedding and I was tempted to just call it off. I wouldn't have this sort of thing; it wasn't fair and I didn't deserve it. He apologized, somewhat, and we went about life as usual. We got married two weeks later in a small church with our family and friends as our guests. One guest specifically, was my cousin, Jenny, who Aaron had gone out with and slept with a couple of years before. He invited her himself. He said they were just friends and dismissed any of my concerns.

Aaron's mom was not pleased that I was marrying her son. I was really hurt to find out she thought I was a bad girl that had trapped her son. She was a religious woman, went to church each Sunday, and believed her son was a good boy. She didn't know he drank or smoked cigarettes. He hid both habits from her well. Her opinion of me just added to my insecurities. I felt like everyone must view me and my family as bad people. My grandpa and grandma had been alcoholics; my mom didn't go to church and sometimes went to the bar. She was a smoker and often went to the café for coffee with my aunts. This certainly didn't make her a bad person in my mind, but in a small community in Utah, if you weren't part of the dominating religion, it seemed you weren't going to fit in as well. Aaron's mom didn't know how I had been raised by my father and that I had been to church each Sunday until the time I moved in with my mom. I still attended once in a while and joined in on some of the youth activities. I actually had quite a spiritual side to me. I prayed often because that was my way of staying close to God. I didn't do drugs, I didn't smoke, and I rarely drank alcohol. I didn't sleep around with everyone and I didn't have a foul mouth. I was a pretty good kid. I tried to dress nice, though I didn't have a lot of clothes, so I did what I could with what I had. I hated that my mom smoked in the house. It made my clothes stink and I was self-conscious about that. I had worked hard on trying to convince everyone I really wasn't a bad girl, and smelling like smoke didn't help. Yes, I considered Aaron's mom's opinion of me to be way off base.

Chapter 4
Marriage

After our wedding, we moved into an apartment closer to the college and Aaron's place of employment. It was different being in a big city on my own. I didn't know where anything was and I hadn't driven a vehicle in traffic like that before. It was kind of a lonely feeling. It didn't help, in fact it added to my misery, that Aaron went out almost every night drinking with his single friends and left me home alone. I lay awake each night he was gone, waiting for the sound of his truck to enter the garage, and all the while my mind would race with worry about him. Would he get in trouble? Would he wreck? What was he out doing? I didn't imagine marriage being like this. I guess I had assumed he would just stop partying and want to spend time with me.

He seemed to love school. He had already been attending for several years, but was still undecided on what he wanted to do. His dad was paying for most of his education and it seemed easy for him to take advantage of that. That was frustrating to me. He had grown up associating money to equal love. He didn't make a lot of money at his job, so we didn't have much of anything. What money we did have, he was always in control of.

I was quite sick with my pregnancy and threw up everyday. I was down in the dumps and it was hard to have any motivation to do anything. I felt really bad that Aaron didn't want to spend time with me. He wanted to go to a play at the college theater with Will's girlfriend, Brandi, but he didn't want me to go with them. I felt like I, being pregnant, must be an embarrassment to him. I let him know I didn't think it was right for him to go with another girl, even if it was with his best friend's girlfriend or for a school assignment; that was the same as a date from my point of view. I didn't like her much either because she wasn't ever friendly to me. He went with her anyway.

Another time, when he did take me with him and his friends, including Will's girlfriend, we were headed to a planetarium. I remember watching as he stared at Brandi as she got out of the truck and walked over to the ATM machine. She was wearing a tight one-piece dress. I felt nothing but coldness from him and was really getting upset with him for not treating me the way I thought he should. As we were walking up to the door of the planetarium, he turned around and sneered at me and called me a slut. That hurt. I was sensitive to being called names, especially that one! I turned around and went back to the truck. I just sat there waiting and hoping he would come back and apologize, which he didn't. I was so embarrassed that he would go in with his friends without me; what had he told them?

Marriage was not easy at age seventeen. I wasn't mature enough to know how to cope with my changing hormones and a husband that would rather be single. My self-esteem was rapidly dropping. He joked about having a threesome with my friend that lived back in our hometown. That made me sick to think of, angry, and insecure about having cute friends. He flirted with other girls often and it didn't matter if I was standing there next to him watching it take place. He would compare me to any cute girl he saw, point out the things he liked about her, and then tell me what I should do different to be more like her. If the girl wasn't cute, he would make fun of her relentlessly. Either way, it was usually about her clothes, make-up, hair, body, job, personality, etc. The message I got: I was not good enough.

As March came, my little brother was not doing well. He finally died of pneumonia after having been in a semi-coma for three years. It was sad, but at the same time it was good that he wasn't suffering anymore. I felt so guilty because I hadn't gone to see him more than once in the couple of months I had been living in the same city as him. I always felt so awkward at the nursing home he lived in. It smelled like weird bubble gum and it was so sad to see the other children there that were suffering in some way too. He shared a room with a little girl that had been severely abused. Her step-grandmother had made her wash her diaper in boiling hot water after she had wet herself, and then hit her in the head with a 2" x 4" board. The side of her head was flat where she had been hit and they had to take skin grafts from her legs to repair her hands. It horrified me to think someone was capable of treating a child that way! The grandma only spent eighteen months in jail. It just wasn't fair!

Aaron drove me back to my mom's house so I could attend my brother's funeral that weekend. However, he said he couldn't go because he had a lot of 'studying' to do. He was angry with me for some reason, as if he had purposely picked a fight, and after I got out of the car, he peeled out of the driveway and left me standing there. I called him several times over the weekend but got no answer.

A few weeks later, I was home in bed late at night when the phone rang. It was Aaron. He had gone to our hometown with his friend, Will. Aaron asked me to come get him right away. I guess it didn't really matter to him that it was the middle of the night and it was a two-hour drive. Apparently, he had confessed to Will that he had slept with his girlfriend, Brandi. Will made him get out of his truck and told him they were no longer friends. Aaron assured me that this had happened with Brandi before we were married. Of course, in Aaron's opinion, that meant it 'didn't count' as cheating on me, and I shouldn't have a right to be upset about it. After that, I didn't like sleeping with him every day like he wanted to because I was feeling pretty troubled about him cheating on me. He said if I didn't want to, he'd go find it somewhere else.

Later on, one evening in April, Aaron and I sat talking in bed. I'm not sure how the conversation started but it ended with more confessions from him. He had slept with Brandi, not only before we were married, but also after, and what's more, he'd slept with her younger sister, Ally, all the while we had been dating. He had taken Brandi to Nevada to gamble and they stayed in a motel together…the weekend of my brother's funeral…that he couldn't attend because he had too much 'studying' to do. It was just unbelievable. How could he do this? He had betrayed me and his best friend, and not to mention it probably hurt Ally too, not that I cared. I cannot describe the pain I felt. He apologized profusely and even got on his knee and promised he would get himself together so we could be sealed in the temple. He wouldn't be able to smoke or drink to be able to do that. This gave me a lot of hope. I thought life would be so much better then. He would stop drinking and partying and I wouldn't have to worry about him cheating on me anymore. Divorce was the last thing I wanted. I didn't want to put my child through that! Aaron told me he had heard about someone from our hometown making a bet that we wouldn't last six months. I was determined to prove them wrong.

He was good for the next couple of weeks but wasn't ready to start the process of changing his habits. I hated it when he drank. He refused to let me drive and he was so irrational. He would yell and argue about anything and go on and on shouting about it. It was best to just agree with him and ignore the behavior so it wouldn't turn into a big fight.

My son was born in July. He was a beautiful baby and I never knew I could be so in love! I was a protective mother and didn't want him out of my sight for a moment. Before I delivered, we moved to a different area of the city, which was also closer to where my older sister lived. She had given birth to my nephew six months earlier, so it was wonderful having her close and getting support and advice on taking care of a baby. My sister and I attended the same college and took our babies to the same caretaker for the fall semester. I worked part time at the college doing secretarial duties. I hated leaving my son with someone else; I wanted him with me all the time! In January, I got a different job and was able to take him with me.

Aaron and I had a couple of incidents during the time we lived in that part of the city. He still came home drunk after being out with his friends all the time. I was so angry and hurt. It was like he was lying to me all over again and wasn't sorry for what he'd done at all. I resented his drinking fiercely. It seemed to be the root of all our problems. I utterly had no trust in him. One night, we had been arguing and he threatened to break my thumbs if I didn't give him the alarm clock. He was twisting them until it hurt. It didn't matter to him that I had to wake up before he did the next morning. He turned the couch upside down looking for it, which really frightened me. I hit him in the shoulder out of anger and frustration. Sometimes our relationship felt more like a fighting brother and sister. He locked me in the bedroom with our sleeping son. I tried to call my sister to come and get me because he was scaring me. He came in and took the phone away and wouldn't allow me to leave. I sat in the bedroom with a plastic toy house in hand in case he came in the room again. He did, and I clonked him on the head with it. It broke the skin on his forehead and started to bleed. He stumbled backwards a few steps and said he couldn't believe I had done that. I felt horrible at the sight of his blood and apologized, but being drunk and irrational as he was, I had been scared of what he might do upon entering the room! We cleaned and bandaged it up and went to bed.

The next morning, he had his friend come over and told him, while I sat right there, that I had hit him with a Tonka truck because I 'was mad at him'. I couldn't believe it. I told him to tell his friend the rest of the story and that it was *not* a Tonka truck, but a plastic toy. He was quite dramatic about the whole thing and went to visit his sister, who was a registered nurse, to see if she thought he needed stitches. A couple of stitches might have helped make it a less noticeable scar, but it was okay without them. I felt really guilty about it and wondered why I was so confused about what had taken place. I wondered how many people he told that I had hit him with a Tonka truck, instead of a plastic toy, because I was 'mad at him'. I wondered if I was in the wrong. I knew hitting wasn't the way to handle things, but that had felt more like self-defense.

We seemed to have a lot of power struggles in our relationship. I am not one to easily allow someone to control me or tell me what I can or cannot do, especially my husband. It really wasn't fair that he wanted to make all the rules for me, but didn't have to follow them himself. I was barely an adult and was trying to find my own identity. It felt like I was living with another 'father'. One day, during my lunch break, I had gone home and we found ourselves in another one of these situations. He slapped me across the face to prove his point. It didn't really hurt physically, but emotionally, it was belittling and hurtful. I was late getting back to work and it was difficult not letting anyone know how unhappy I was.

Aaron finally came to a point where he wanted to prepare himself to go through the temple. We took a class together and life seemed to get better. He wasn't drinking, and that made all the difference to me. He was more humble, I felt like I could trust him again, and it was easier for us to get along. I had always been taught that I needed to go through the temple to have my family sealed together. Subconsciously, I thought when you reached that point, life would be perfect. It was not.

We moved to another apartment not too far from our old one. It was less expensive, and being college students, that was better for us. We got into another power struggle one day and I was being sassy. Aaron kicked me in the back as I walked away from him toward the kitchen, then he put me in a headlock and dragged me into the living room. He sat on top of me choking me, and all the while my son stood there watching and screaming. He was only a year old and I'm sure it was quite frightening for him to see his parents behaving like that! I scratched at Aaron's neck and pulled on his shirt trying to get him off me. His button broke and he sat back, came to his senses, and then got up. He went and looked in the mirror and came back saying, "Look what you did to my neck! Look what you did to my shirt! You need to fix this button!" I apologized and fixed the button. I was so upset that my son had witnessed such horrific behavior and that Aaron had literally acted as if he might kill me. I didn't believe he really would, I knew he was just really angry, but I made up my mind right then that I was leaving him as soon as I had the chance. When Aaron left for work, I got my son and we drove to my parent's house about three hours away.

Aaron called me sometime after I arrived at my parent's house wanting to know what I was doing. After a few days, he eventually talked me into coming back. I was mortified to find out he had told his friends and family that I 'wigged out and went to my parent's house', as if I was just a crazy person. Of course, *he* had nothing at all to do with it and wouldn't take any responsibility for his part. I was just a girl with 'emotional problems'. He often told me he thought I had a hormone imbalance and that I should get some medicine for it, which made me feel pretty stupid and a bit angry. It seemed like to me he was using that as a scapegoat for his behavior and my reactions. Maybe I *did* have a hormone imbalance, I didn't know, but I didn't like feeling like everything was my fault and it really upset me that he wouldn't take any accountability for his actions. At the time, I didn't understand this, I didn't know how to explain and put into words what I felt. That lack of communication and maturity was not helpful in trying to repair our damaged relationship. I was no match for Aaron; he was superior in his skills with debate and dominated all of our arguments. He might have made a great lawyer.

We moved back to our hometown so I would be near both of our families while Aaron began his training for the army. He was in Texas for three months and then we planned to go to another college town to finish our schooling. Life seemed to be going well, until we moved.

This college town was beautiful, but it was full of single students, many that liked to party. Aaron went over to his friend's apartment quite often and started up his old ways again. They all drank, so he did too. It must have been difficult for him not having any married friends, although he didn't try to seek them out. I seemed to really cramp his style. I did go with him to his friend's apartment a few times and met some of the other college kids that lived in the same apartment complex, but I felt out of place and didn't like having my child there. It wasn't exactly a kid-friendly environment.

Super Bowl weekend came around and we were visiting our families in our hometown. Aaron and I were driving around and talking when the conversation turned to him putting my family down, again. He never had anything nice to say about any of them. He seemed to think he and his family were all better than everyone else. I was getting so upset that I asked him to pull the car over and let me out. He wouldn't stop. He continued bashing my family. When he made the comment so snidely that my family was just 'full of child abusers and molesters', I punched him and screamed at him to let me out of the car! With that, he immediately pulled over and told me to get out, which I did gladly! I walked to my mom's house in the dark. He drove by a few times looking for me, but I hid whenever I saw our car coming. Harsh and cruel words leave deep wounds and they are not easy to take back. He left me at my mom's and went back home.

When I returned home, he had another confession for me. He had a hard time with his conscience eating at him, sometimes anyway, when he couldn't justify it to himself. He had been with another girl over the weekend. He said they did everything except actually sleep together. It was pretty much all the same to me. I was even more livid that I had met the girl the previous week and she was fully aware that I was married and had a child with Aaron. I left. I just needed to get away. I was so angry and had so much pent up emotion! I went to the apartment where the girl lived and waited for her to come home. We stood outside her door and I confronted her about what she and my husband had done. She told me he said he was getting divorced. I hit her right in the face, more than once, and yelled at her to stay away from my husband or else!

I had never been in a fight before, unless you count the time when I was ten years old and got into a tiff with the annoying neighbor girl. She was constantly walking right into our house, uninvited, and helping herself to our food and television. My older sister turned on her stereo and played 'Eye of the Tiger' when she found us arguing. I was having a really hard time keeping a straight face with the Rocky music in the background. I think we wrestled around on the lawn for a minute but I was laughing most of the time. She finally called me a gorilla and stormed home. My older sister and I were rolling with laughter after she left. I was a *gorilla,* of all things.

I left the girl's apartment building and headed straight to Josie's house. She was living in the same town as me and also attended college there. I told her what had happened and we went for a drive up the canyon to talk. I couldn't believe what I had done to that poor girl. She was just a dumb girl that wanted attention from whoever would give it to her. She probably didn't think about how her actions would affect me and my marriage. Why was I so mad at her anyway? *Aaron* was the one I should have been mad at.

After talking with Josie and cooling down, I headed back home. Aaron was still there waiting for me. I told him what had taken place earlier in the evening and he seemed to actually be flattered and just laughed about it. He warned me that the police could show up at our house at any time and explained how what I had done was illegal and that the girl could press charges. In my mind, I almost dared her to try and press charges! I didn't understand how what I had done was illegal; it seemed more like a natural consequence from my point of view. If you mess with my family, you're going to get it. I had no idea that there was actually a law against making threats to harm someone or for hitting someone. I didn't know much about the law, that's for sure. No cops ever came to our door, and the girl stayed far away from me. I still felt bad for her. I had flowers sent to her apartment a year later. I didn't like grudges and I didn't like knowing I had hurt someone and just wanted to try to make things right on my part.

Aaron and I didn't get along too well over the next few months. He thought he should take the car to school and to work and that I should walk. Both places were only a few blocks away, so it wasn't a huge deal, it just made me feel like he always came first. One day we got into an argument and I locked him out of the house. He was really scaring me! He kicked the front door open, which broke the lock, and the next thing I knew I was on my knees begging him not to hit me. He didn't, but his fist was raised and he was ready to. I tried to leave but he got on the hood of the car. I drove down the road a short distance and stopped so he would get off. I didn't actually want to hurt him. He took the keys and the car, and left.

He invited an old fling of his over to study and went to study with her at her house sometimes too. He teased me and made fun of me while she was at our house; it seemed I was always the butt of his jokes around his friends. I would tell him I didn't like it, only to be met with another dispute about me being too sensitive and emotional. He also said that of me when I had gotten upset with him for going for a drive up the canyon with her. I shouldn't have been troubled by that, in Aaron's opinion, because nothing had happened between them. I believed it was only because *she* hadn't allowed it to go that far. I still wasn't happy with her for going on a drive alone with my husband. I felt she should've known better than that! Aaron's outlook on being around old girlfriends was certainly not shared by me. He seemed to think it was ok to go visit them, without me of course. He looked up my cousin, Jenny, when he went to the town she was living in and then went and met with her. He had talked about her a lot and I knew he still had feelings for her. She became his 3rd wife later on down the road. They were only married for about three months. I always wondered if anything had happened between them when he went to see her during the time we were married.

Aaron had a job as a lifeguard at the public swimming pool. Some days I didn't know where he was when he was off work and he didn't have the courtesy to let me know. It was getting close to summer again and he had been spending a lot of time at work or just gone. He came home late one evening and I could tell he had been drinking. He was so cold towards me. I pressured him to talk to me and tell me where he had been. He didn't want to tell me anything for quite some time. He said he just wanted to get a divorce. I felt so devastated. He didn't even want to talk about it. I left that night and went to my mom's. I called him each day for the next month. He would almost never answer, and if he did, he wanted to get off the phone quickly. I found out he had a girlfriend basically living there with him and she had moved in the day after I left. She worked with him at the swimming pool.

I was so lost. I didn't know what to do anymore. I couldn't stand other girls. They were all a threat to me.

My son and I lived with my mom during that summer. I didn't eat much, because I had no appetite. I didn't realize that I was losing so much weight. I worked when I could and played at the reservoir with my little boy. I hung out with Aaron's little sister sometimes and she introduced me to Ian. Ian treated me like a queen. I knew he really liked me, but I was still in love with Aaron. I kept trying to call Aaron, but it was always to no avail. I finally caved and went out with Ian. I just didn't care anymore. I was hurting so much and felt so rejected. I just wanted to be loved again and I wanted the pain to go away. I found that the quickest way to numb my feelings and forget about Aaron and his girlfriend was to go out with someone else.

After a couple of months had gone by, Aaron came to visit. I sat outside on the porch with him and we had a good talk. I missed him. I didn't think he'd want to get back together with me because I had been with someone else. I told him what I had done and he was absolutely astonished. He said he never imagined I would do something like that. He still wanted me back. He went straight home and made his girlfriend leave our house, then he went and talked with his bishop to try and get himself right again. He called me each day and told me he was reading scriptures and doing things to 'repent'. I was reluctant to follow in his footsteps. I felt guilt and shame for what I had done, but I was afraid to break it off with Ian because I knew it would hurt him. However, I knew it was the right thing to do and I didn't love him. I hated making others feel bad, even when trying to keep them happy was at my own expense. I didn't realize at the time that there was a word for that. It's called codependency.

Codependency: unhealthy love and a tendency to behave in overly passive or excessively caretaking ways that negatively impact one's relationships and quality of life. It also often involves placing a lower priority on one's own needs, while being excessively preoccupied with the needs of others. Codependency can occur in any type of relationship, including in families, at work, in friendships, and also in romantic, peer or community relationships. Codependency may also be characterized by denial, low self-esteem, excessive compliance, and/or control patterns. Narcissists are considered to be natural magnets for the codependent.

- Wikipedia

I broke it off with Ian and went back to Aaron soon after. Things were great and life seemed fine again. It was good to be home, but I still had some resentment towards Aaron, and I didn't fully trust him. I didn't believe divorce was the best option though, and if he was willing to try and make it work, then so was I. We planned to have another child, as if that would seal our marriage and somehow help make things better. I got pregnant within a week of going off my birth control. It was exciting! I really wanted my son to have a brother or sister to play with and I didn't want him to be an only child.

I still had a quiet nagging in the back of my mind about Ian. I had really hurt him. I wanted to tell him I was sorry for putting him through all that and somehow ease his pain as a friend would. I never should have gone out with him in the first place. I called and talked with him on the phone. I knew Aaron wouldn't like me talking to Ian, but I did it anyway.

We went to our hometown one weekend and Aaron wanted to go hang out with his friend, Jackson. Jackson had recently divorced my good friend Kathy, and I didn't like him much. He wasn't someone I thought Aaron should be hanging out with because I was afraid he'd get into trouble with him, but as usual, Aaron did what he wanted. I had some free time, and wasn't too happy with Aaron not caring how I felt, so I went to see Ian. I just wanted to talk to him and somehow try to cheer him up a little, strictly as a friend. I knew this was wrong and that Aaron would disprove, but he seemed to think it was okay to go see old girlfriends, so what was the big deal? I just wouldn't tell him and no harm would be done. I was obviously acting on a passive aggressive motive by not caring how it would make Aaron feel, but was not consciously aware of that at the time. I also seemed to think if *I* did what *he'd* done by going to see an ex, then I couldn't be mad at him for it anymore.

Aaron wanted to run for president of the college we were attending and he and some others formed a group for their campaign. He spent a lot of time together with them making signs and advertising for votes. I was excited for him to be doing something that made him feel good about himself. It was a bit challenging having him gone all the time, and I felt a little uneasy about the fact that everyone in his group was single except him. I just didn't want him to put himself in any position that would jeopardize our relationship, which he seemed to have a knack for.

Aaron found out I had talked to Ian on the phone and that I had gone to see him. He was rather upset with me. I promised him that nothing had happened and told him my reason for going.

He seemed to forgive me, but soon he started accusing me of cheating on him and telling other people that he didn't know if the child I was carrying was his. He was drinking all the time again and would be gone for the entire day and not come home until after midnight sometimes. At one point, he told me it was *my* fault that he drank...I 'drove him to drinking'. I really felt like he was using my mistakes against me to make himself feel better about what he was doing and to make others feel sorry for him. That really hurt. I was already carrying a tremendous load of guilt; it didn't matter what the circumstances were that led me to do the things I did, I knew better. But for him to say our baby might not be his was just too much. Aaron always expected me to forgive him for his mistakes, and didn't like having them brought up, so why was it okay for him to do this to me? He was so unfair! I just wanted to scream sometimes!

One day, I was waiting for Aaron at school while he was visiting with other students about the campaign, when his ex-girlfriend pulled up in her car. She smiled really big at him, and he smiled back even bigger. I felt sick. To make matters worse, he walked over to her window and starting talking to her, all the while I was standing there watching and he knew it, and obviously didn't care at all. I asked him what he was doing and it was almost as if he was angry with me for even asking. I was 'being too sensitive'. I stormed off. I just thought he was unbelievable. It wasn't okay for me to talk to my ex, but it was okay for him. I got in my car and left. I literally wanted to die. I contemplated how I would commit suicide. I couldn't though, because I was pregnant and had a beautiful little boy. I didn't know how to cope with my life. It all felt crazy.

It wasn't long before he had another girlfriend again. I moved out and went to live near my dad and stepmom. It was such a difficult time being pregnant and going through this at the same time. However, I was grateful for being pregnant; it helped give me good reason to take care of myself. I was starting over and trying to get going in school again. I had a duplex out in the country and it seemed I could actually do it on my own.

Aaron came to pick up our son for Easter vacation and I ended up going with him on the trip. We did a lot of talking on the long drive and decided to get back together again. I moved all of my stuff back to our old house.

Life was great for about a week. They call this the 'honeymoon phase' of a relationship. It's when the relationship feels new and exciting again. It can last longer than a week, sometimes months, but not this time.

Aaron worked part time in the college's circuit weight training room during the spring. Sometimes, after I finished my classes, I would go over and do the circuit and visit with him for a few minutes. One day when I went there, I found him chatting with a beautiful girl. She had long curly blonde hair and an athletic build. This seemed to be Aaron's favorite 'type'. He introduced me to her as his friend, Crystal, but it was dispiriting to watch as he looked her up and down longingly. I felt fat and ugly being in my third trimester of pregnancy and this didn't lessen my anguish. I often tried explaining to him how awful it made me feel when he flirted or stared at other girls, and especially when he would actually point out what he admired about them and proceed to compare me to them and tell me what I should do different to be more like them, but he just said he couldn't help it and that I was too sensitive. He would tell me he was just trying to help me be the best I could be. It's sad to me now that I could weigh 125 pounds at 5'7" after having my first child and still be told I needed to work out more to tone up. Sure, we can all improve and look better with more effort. Why wasn't he a body builder then? He could have done that with some more effort. Why didn't he suntan more often and dress like a million bucks all the time? Why didn't he have perfect hair? I didn't marry him for his looks; that's why. He was okay looking, not what I would call gorgeous, but he was likeable in appearance. People's personalities definitely make all the difference. A less fortunate looking person can be dazzling if they are personable, and a gorgeous person can be quite unattractive with a superficial personality.

I soon came to realize that Aaron only wanted me when he didn't have me, and once he had me again, he didn't really want me anymore. Someone else would always seem more attractive and enticing. He became extremely cold toward me as the next few weeks went by. It hurt tremendously that I had moved all my stuff out and started over, then moved it all back, only to be rejected again. I moved back to my same duplex near my parents. This was all quite distressing to go through while being pregnant. My cousin, Josie, said her friend saw Aaron kissing that girl he'd introduced me to in the weight room the day after I moved out. They had been just outside the college library, for all to see. I was devastated. I felt worthless, depressed, and like I surely would never be good enough.

I started back to school and got my life going again. I was grateful to have the love and support from my family to help me get through that hard time.

When the day came to deliver my second son, I called Aaron to let him know I was having our baby. I didn't expect him to come, but he did. I had mixed feelings towards him, but he was kind and it felt good to have him near during the delivery. I told him he could stay at my house with our older son while I was at the hospital. We visited for a while before he left and I was under the impression that he wanted to get back together again. He had been sweet and flirtatious with me. He asked me to call him when I awoke the next morning, and then he would come back to the hospital.

I called the next morning, several times, to find my line busy for over an hour and a half. It was quite discouraging. Who could he be talking to for so long? As it turns out, he had been talking to his girlfriend, Crystal. My heart ached. I couldn't keep doing this. I returned home to find my house a mess. I would think after letting him stay at my house, he would at least clean up after himself, especially since I just had a baby! Why was he so disrespectful and rude? I was finally starting to see him for who he really was. He was selfish and self-centered. He would never be capable of fully loving me. It was time to end the relationship we had been in now for four years. Shortly after he left, we filed for a divorce.

I felt pretty depressed when I went to my two-week post-baby checkup. My doctor put me on an anti-depressant again.

As fall came, I went to visit my mom and some of my relatives in my other hometown. They were encouraging me to move on with my life and start dating again. I wasn't sure if I was ready for that and my divorce hadn't been finalized yet. I went to watch some baseball games while I was there and this guy asked me if I wanted to go out with him. I was reluctant, but my cousin insisted that I should just go and have fun. He was attentive and polite, a nice change from what I had been used to. Over the next few months, we talked on the phone and wrote letters to each other often. It was good to have someone to talk to and laugh with. I invited him to come with me to a friend's wedding, and he stayed at my house. The plan was that he would sleep on the couch, but that isn't what happened. Again, I felt guilt and shame because I wasn't officially divorced yet. I knew better. Why was that such a challenge for me? I had to ask myself if this was really the kind of girl I was. Depending on who I talked to, there were different opinions on the matter. Some would say it was wrong, some would say it was no big deal. What did *I* think? I believed it was right to only be with one person, and be *married* to that person. That was easier said than done under the circumstances. As it goes, long distance relationships are hard to keep up, and we broke it off. I knew he really wasn't right for me anyway. We didn't believe in all the same things, and part of me was still trying to figure out what it was that I did believe.

It was really difficult being a single mom. I didn't enjoy the status of it at all. I wanted to be married and have a complete family. It was lonely and financially challenging. Aaron came to visit the boys and I let him stay with me. Our divorce still hadn't been finalized and it felt good to be all together as a family. It was just not possible for me to say goodbye to him. I had given him my whole heart and it wasn't easy to let him go. It wasn't long before he came to live with us again.

Aaron had been in college for seven years up to that point, and still had no degree and didn't know what he wanted to do. He talked about wanting to be a police officer, but his dad wanted him to be an electrical engineer. I convinced him that he needed to do *something* and it would be good if it was a job he would enjoy. He joined the police academy and got a job shortly thereafter. He seemed quite content in that line of work, and life didn't feel so much like a rollercoaster for the next year and a half. I worked as a youth tracker and tutor and occasionally babysat for other people. It didn't matter; in Aaron's eyes, I wasn't making enough money and he wanted me to bring in more income. I tried to explain to him that daycare would be expensive and the jobs I had were perfect because I could set my own hours. It was always an issue. I did work off and on during the time we were together, but I think he wanted me to do something more permanent and full time. It was so hard to raise and take care of two small children, attend college, and have a job too. Also, I was raised to believe that one parent should stay home with the children. I don't really understand why he didn't feel that way; he had been raised that way too. His mom was a full-time homemaker and his dad provided their income. Aaron didn't like it when I spent money, which was something I didn't do often, but one time, he locked the checkbooks up in his filing cabinet and wouldn't let me have them because I had spent more than he wanted me to. He then changed the account to only show his name on the checks. He said he 'didn't mean to do that' and just laughed about it, but didn't change it back with my name included. Another issue we had was concerning his truck. He had gotten a new truck during our separation and he said I couldn't drive it. He wanted to save the miles on it and then re-sell it. *He* could drive it though. It just seemed typical of him to not let me do something he could do, and everything of any value was always going to be 'his'.

Although I didn't believe he cheated on me during this time of our marriage, he continued his flirting and I still felt like I was never good enough or would measure up to his standards of what I should look and act like or do as a career. I never fully trusted him and still had some resentment in the back of my mind. He always had to be 'right' about everything and there was no use in arguing once he had his mind set. I didn't like the way he teased me either. It was constant and belittling. He would often call me a 'stick in the mud' or tell me I was 'too sensitive'.

The thing that hurt the most was his indifference to our boys. He wasn't unkind to them or anything; it was just as if he didn't know how to connect with them. When he came home from work he just wanted them to go play in their room. He came first and he acted like what he wanted was always more important than what the kids wanted. Our second son was eight months old when he finally changed his first diaper. Granted, we were separated for the majority of that time, but he didn't try to visit them much or seem too concerned about them. He was a bit distant from our second son. They hadn't really had an opportunity to bond. I tried to reassure him that he *was* in fact his child. I swore to him that I had not cheated on him. I pointed out a couple of things to help the matter; they had the same rare blood type and he *looked* like him. I still felt like he was just using it as an excuse to make others look down on me and feel sorry for him. It seemed he needed something to hold over me to make me feel guilty and for him to be able to punish me with.

I found myself constantly praying for an answer as to whether or not I should get divorced. I didn't want to do the wrong thing. I just felt like God wasn't going to tell me what to do. Why wouldn't He just give me a clear answer?

Back in high school, there was a boy that I had put up on a pedestal thinking he was perfect. He went to church and was a pretty good kid. He was athletic, got good grades, and had a lot of friends. Everyone liked him. I was continually disappointed that he wasn't interested in me back then. It crushed me. Why wasn't I good enough for this boy? If I liked someone, it seemed I had always been able to make my way into their heart. I think I enjoyed the challenge, but this one never gave in. As a matter of fact, he never really dated anyone. In my mind, it gave me even more reason to prove I was a 'good girl' so he would like me. It never occurred to me that he might not really be perfect. For some reason, I made it into something much bigger than it ever should have been. I *had* to get him to like me somehow. I *needed* to be accepted by this person that wouldn't give me the time of day. All I managed to do was make myself miserable and gave myself a warped interpretation of what he and others must think of me. I was never able to show them who I really was. I knew that once a person got to know me, we'd have a ton of fun and our friendship would be great. It was getting to that point that was the hard part. I had lots of acquaintances. A lot of kids seemed to think I was rather humorous. I was, when I felt comfortable around them. I was quite surprised and flattered at how many boys had come forward during my separation from Aaron and told me they had had a crush on me in high school. I hadn't the slightest idea. It was a nice boost to my self-esteem and helped me realize that the notion I had about what others thought of me was untrue.

I had it in the back of my mind that if I got divorced from Aaron, I would look up this guy from my high school and see if he would be interested in me. I thought my life would be better with someone like him instead. I don't know why, but I still had that awful concept in my head that if he accepted me, it meant I was good enough.

Summer was almost over and Aaron decided he wanted to make a road trip to his parent's house…without me. It also happened to be where his ex-girlfriend lived. I knew he wanted to go see her. I begged him to let me go with him and all I got was a firm 'no' and the door slammed as he left me sitting on the couch crying. I was just devastated. I couldn't believe how heartless and cold he could be.

When he returned from his trip, he admitted to stopping in our old college town and visiting his friends, including another old girlfriend, and then going to his parent's house in the next town over. He confessed to going to see his ex-girlfriend, Crystal, and going for a drive with her. He seemed angry with me and was rather bitter over the next several weeks. He said nothing happened between them and that she was engaged. I wondered if that had made him unhappy.

My birthday came the next month. I reminded him the day before, but he got up early the next morning and left to go to work, stayed late, came home and changed to go running, and then left again without a word. He didn't get home until after I had finally gone to bed. It was as if he had purposely gone out of his way to make me feel bad on my birthday. A couple of weeks later, I came home from the store to find him baking cookies with our older son and there was a new vacuum in the living room. He said they were making cookies for me for my birthday and the vacuum was my birthday present. I really didn't know what to think. I was rather confused. Why bother at this point?

We had some road construction going on near where we lived and Aaron told me about a girl that worked with the crew. He said they sat and visited as she held the stop sign. I got a sick feeling, because in the past, my gut usually told me when something wasn't right in these kinds of situations. Would she be the next girl he'd cheat on me with?

I just couldn't do this anymore. We argued a lot and it seemed we just hated each other. I didn't trust him. I was so hurt that he would go see his ex-girlfriend, Crystal, the one that he left me for when I was pregnant and in my third trimester, the one he had been seen kissing outside the college library the day after I left, and yes, the one that seemed to be everything I wasn't. I was so tired of being second, and never good enough.

Divorce

We decided to get divorced after six years of marriage. He moved out and moved into another duplex two houses down the street. He still came over to my house a few times, but when I didn't want to do anything with him, he left.

I went over to one of my friend's house once and she had invited several others over. It was a small party, and the girl from the construction crew was there. Somebody asked me my name and when she heard me say my last name, she asked if I was married to Aaron. I told her I had been, and she freaked out and ran into the other room. I didn't find out what that was all about, but it wasn't hard to guess. It was really difficult to see him dating other girls, and I felt a strong desire to leave that town and go back to live near my mom. Aaron didn't ever really try to see the boys either, which I thought was pretty sad since he only lived two houses away, so I figured moving to another town wouldn't be too detrimental on him.

I looked up the guy from high school, and of course he still wasn't interested in me. This sort of confirmed to me that I was not good enough for someone like him. I felt so vulnerable and so worthless after my divorce. I hated being a 'single parent', though I absolutely adored my two boys. I just felt incomplete and on my own. It really was hard. I felt like giving up sometimes but just kept moving forward, kind of on auto-pilot.

Over the next several months, I worked a lot of hours for little money and then spent my free time playing in the sun and water at the reservoir with my boys or going out with my friends. I drank sometimes and didn't really care about trying to be good anymore.

Chapter 5

Dusty

"The first time someone shows you who they are, believe them." - Maya Angelou

I had a lot of relatives in the small town I was living in, and many of them had horses. Summer was a fun time for rodeos and going to the arenas. I loved watching my uncles rope calves. I had grown up going and helping them by opening the chute and warming up and cooling down the horses, but my favorite rodeo event was the bull riding. It was intense and exciting! The only thing I had ever done that came anywhere close to bull riding was when I had ridden some calves a couple of times. I think I lasted about two or three seconds each time before I fell off. They didn't buck; they just ran out of the chute rather swiftly. It was fun! At one particular rodeo, some young bronc riders came over and introduced themselves. I wasn't really excited to enter into a serious relationship, so I acted a bit snobbish toward them. However, I did give my phone number to one. He had beautiful blue eyes, a great smile, and seemed quite sure of himself.

A few weeks passed when he finally called me. I wasn't holding my breath or anything, so I was surprised to hear from him. He apologized several times for having misplaced my phone number and said he called as soon as he found it. He was kind and offered to come back and take me out to dinner. I told him he couldn't stay at my house if he did. He was from Salt Lake, and I didn't know him at all. We visited on the phone several times and talked for lengthy periods before we started officially dating. We talked about so many things. He told me his goals and about his life working on ranches and training horses. He was currently in the business of horse shoeing. He said he had been married before and had a daughter, but said he was unable to have any more children due to a bronc riding accident. He went on to explain that he'd gone to the doctor and was told that he was sterile. He later lived with a girl in Idaho for quite some time and tried to have kids with her, but was unable to. He said she filed common law marriage earlier that spring, but it had only lasted two weeks before they split up and had it annulled.

My good friend, Nicole, didn't like him. She said he was no fun. He was such a serious person. I enjoyed the challenge of trying to make him smile and laugh. It wasn't that difficult to do. He seemed to really like me and was a gentleman. I disregarded her opinion and thought maybe he was good for me because he seemed stable and knew what he wanted in life. He rarely drank and was quite convincing that he was not the cheating type, both of which were a huge deal to me. I didn't ever want to be with someone that liked drinking or that would cheat on me again.

I had been living in a house that my mom owned, but she was planning on selling it, so I would have to find another place to live when she did. I didn't think my life was going to get any better staying in the small town I was in and contemplated going back to college. My plan was to move back to Salt Lake City so I could finish my degree.

Dusty offered to help me move, which I thought was wonderful! I went to visit him in Salt Lake where he was currently staying with his grandma. He and his grandma were close. She was almost like his mother. She had a small ranch that he was helping her take care of. She was a minister in her church, and her ranch was actually a ministry. She occasionally took other people in when they needed a home and helped them get back on their feet. She had another house in Salt Lake that she used as a storage place. It was full of donation items that she would box together and give to people in need. She was quite a woman and a hard worker. She went to church and read her bible. She didn't watch regular television; the only television shows allowed in her house were Christian programs. For being a ministry, the ranch sure didn't feel peaceful. I found it to be anything but that.

The first time I stayed there with him while his grandma was there (she went out of town a lot), he yelled at me for turning off his alarm clock and was rather rude to me for not making him some breakfast. I didn't feel comfortable getting up and cooking in his grandma's kitchen and the idea hadn't even crossed my mind. If anything, he should have been making *me* breakfast. He complained and said I should just make myself at home there. I thought he was ridiculous and knew then that he wasn't someone I wanted to be with. Unfortunately, I found out I was pregnant later that day, which was rather surprising considering the fact that he was 'sterile and unable to have children'. It was then that he informed me that the doctor had told him to come back six months after their visit to get re-checked, but he didn't do the follow-up. That would have been some nice information earlier. I wondered if he had ever even been to the doctor, or even in a bronc riding accident for that matter.

After he found out I was pregnant, he was excited and begged me to let him be a part of his baby's life. He promised to help me pay for everything and to help take care of me. He said he would help me get an apartment, but I told him I didn't believe in living together unmarried. He was okay with that, and said he wouldn't live there. I soon discovered that just because he said a thing, it did not mean he truly meant it. I began to see the 'real' Dusty and he wasn't anything like the person I thought he was.

I moved into an apartment under his name because I didn't have the proper income and work history to qualify there. He would come over and then try to make me feel guilty about having him leave. After a while, that turned into him refusing to leave because 'it was *his* apartment and *he* was paying the rent'. I didn't go to school as planned, and I didn't get a job. I was really sick and depressed. I didn't want to get a job because I wanted to leave and couldn't easily do that if I was tied down to a job.

I was so scared of being tied to him that I actually considered having an abortion. I had never really understood what that entirely entailed. I didn't realize that the baby had a beating heart so soon and was actually a little person growing inside me. The ultrasound tech said I was further along than I had originally thought, so I didn't want to go through with it. I had already been wavering on the whole idea anyway. It turned out I wasn't further along, but I consider that to be an *enormous* blessing. I would never have been able to forgive myself if I had done it. I learned more about what it actually meant to me and I was strongly against it after that. I know that there are certain cases where it may need to be done, but in my opinion, the circumstances would need to be extreme (a danger to the mother's health, or sometimes as a result of rape/incest) and with *a lot* of prayer and consideration.

Five months into the relationship, it came out that Dusty was 'technically still married'. I was furious! I was entirely opposed to that. I couldn't believe he had lied to me about something so serious! He said it wasn't a big deal. He said his 'wife' that filed common law marriage on him, was supposed to have it annulled, but he had simply not checked up on it to make sure it had been done. I *really* didn't want to be there with him after that and felt enormous guilt about it, so I left almost every other weekend. I always ended up going back because he would call and cry and beg me to stay with him. He would promise to do better and change the way he acted. He would buy me flowers and be really sweet for a short while after I returned, but he always ended up acting badly again. He was *so* persuasive and convincing on the phone and I always got sucked into looking at things from his point of view. I started feeling like I was getting brainwashed.

I made the mistake of confiding in Dusty about having considered getting an abortion early in my pregnancy. I told him I wasn't sure if it was his because I might have been further along than I had thought. I had been with someone else the month before I started seeing Dusty. I remember *wishing* I had been further along so I wouldn't have any obligation to stay with him!

Dusty had gotten mad at me one night in January because I had 'attitude' and said he was calling my dad to come and get me. Attitude, in his opinion, was when I stood up for myself and what I believed in or disagreed with. I gave him Aaron's phone number instead of my dad's because I didn't want him upsetting my dad like that. I thought Aaron was my friend and could help me somehow if I needed him to, despite our differences we had when we'd been married. When he asked what my dad's name was again, I said 'Aaron'. I didn't care if it made him mad; I was tired of him treating me so badly and I was tired of his insane accusations! He was jealous of the attention I gave my boys and tried to keep them from sitting next to me on the couch. It seemed he was jealous of anything that took attention away from him. He used really awful language and was so hateful to everyone around him. I found him to be racist, egotistical, arrogant, hypocritical, controlling, possessive, and a liar. He didn't respect my religion. He made fun of it and put me down constantly. He didn't like my family or friends and put all of them down also. I didn't realize it at the time, but he was trying to isolate me from everyone that cared about me.

He ripped the phone out of the wall and told me to get in the other room if I didn't want the boys to watch us fight. He pushed me as I was walking down the hall and then threw the phone at me. It hit my leg and left a big bruise. He pushed me down on the bed and accused me of sleeping with Aaron and told me I was a wh---. He was verbally abusive for a while and then, a while later, he said he was sorry.

The following day, we got into a bigger fight. Dusty was sick (as usual) and came home from work early. He usually made himself sick by worrying that I would leave him after he'd been so mean. I was planning to go to my cousin's wedding that night in my hometown, but Dusty wanted me to stay home with him. I didn't think he was that sick, but I said I would go to the wedding and then come right back. He got really mad because he didn't think I cared about him. He told me to give him the house key. I told him no, because it was my apartment, and shut the bathroom door and locked it. He broke the door down with his foot, so I just handed him the key. I didn't want to fight, especially in the confinement of the bathroom, and being five months pregnant! He pushed me around a lot that night and wouldn't let me leave. At one point he tried to make me leave without my shoes on. At another point in time, he was going to keep my car keys and make me leave on foot. During that moment, I was so frustrated with him for holding me against my will, that I started slapping at his arms. He pushed me into the kitchen and kicked me in the back. He said he was "going to take the baby right now" and picked up a glass. He punched the wall next to my face and broke the picture hanging on the wall behind me. I knew he wasn't going to let me leave and I was scared. He pushed me into the bedroom and hit me upside the back of my head. I told him I was going to call the cops. He said, "Fine, but you'll be dead before they get here."

That made me quite nervous but I kind of laughed and nonchalantly said, "That's funny, I've never been threatened to be killed before."

"I wouldn't really do anything; go ahead and call," he replied smugly. So I did! I tried not to sound upset on the phone because I wanted Dusty to think I was just bluffing. Unfortunately, the 911 personnel didn't take me seriously. When Dusty figured out that I had actually called 911, he came over and yanked the phone cord out of the wall and shouted at me to leave before the cops got there. As I was leaving, I could hear him breaking my stereo in my bedroom.

I went to the nearest gas station and asked if I could possibly get some gas without paying. I was desperate; I had no money, and was paranoid that Dusty would follow me. He told me earlier that night (when he was going to make me leave without anything) that he was going to follow me to make sure I didn't go somewhere else or make any phone calls. My car was on empty but he said he didn't care about that or if it left me stranded out in the middle of nowhere.

Luckily, a lady said she would put a small amount of gas in my car for me. I was crying and hysterical. I told her I was afraid my boyfriend would follow me, and graciously thanked her. I went straight to my hometown praying the whole way that I would make it and not run out of gas, and kept checking to make sure he wasn't actually following me. I went to my cousin's wedding and found my mom and explained to her what had happened.

I moved in with her that weekend. I didn't talk to Dusty for a couple of weeks, but I saw him again around Valentine's Day. I had gone to give the boys to Aaron, and Dusty wanted me to come back through Salt Lake to see him and said he had a Valentine gift for me. I went to my hometown instead. However, later the next night, I gave in and decided to go see him. I hit a deer on the way, but thankfully made it to the apartment. I had no choice but to leave my car there. The front end was crunched in and it was barely running. When I knocked on the door, he answered and seemed quite surprised that it was me. He said he had been at the bar earlier that night and that he thought a girl he had kissed on the dance floor followed him home. I wasn't too upset about it; after all, I left him. My cousin ended up picking me up and taking me to get my boys and then took me to meet my mom. Everyone was really mad that I had gone to see him.

For a week, I stayed with my mom in her apartment with her and my youngest sister and my two boys until I could get my own apartment. It was nice to have my own place to do as I pleased, but more importantly, it felt safe.

I talked on the phone with Dusty every now and again over the next few months. He was always trying to convince me that he could change and would try to make me feel guilty about not letting him be a part of his baby's life by staying with him. We were sort of in the process of working on our relationship. He came to the hospital when my daughter was born, but I was frustrated with him because he wouldn't let my mom and Nicole come in the room with me. He wanted to be the only one there. I really wanted them in there too, but he said he would leave forever if I let them. I couldn't have been that lucky.

On the day I brought her home from the hospital, I had to ask Dusty to leave. He was seriously upsetting me and I didn't want him at my house. He said he would leave, but was taking his baby with him. With that, he packed her up and headed out the door. He told me I was never going to see him or her ever again. I panicked and started crying uncontrollably! What could I do but sit there? I was in pain and was in no condition to run after him. I had just come home from giving birth and was nursing her. He just couldn't take my newborn baby away like that! I begged him to stay and told him I *wanted* him to stay with me. It was the only thing that would keep him from leaving with her. He said if I ever left with her, I better never come back. He said he'd come and get her and kill anyone that got between him and his daughter. Another time, he said he would kill *me* if *I* got in the way, and if I did run with her, then I better keep running. He said the most dreadful things sometimes. I believe he said them only to cause fear in me and to make him feel like he was in control, but I doubted he would really ever follow through on any of his threats. How could I take that chance and be sure?

He often spoke of killing his ex-wife and said things like 'I should have killed her while I had the chance. I should have put a pair of cement shoes on her and threw her in the river', and 'if only I could be alone with her for ten minutes'. Once, he said that he could be logged in as driving truck in his logbook, take a rent-a-car to come back and kill her, and no one would ever even know. Their marriage hadn't been any better than ours. He said he was ignoring her one time, so she threw a cast-iron skillet at him. When he came to, he put her in a chokehold and told her to never hit him again. She told me that once he'd held a knife to her throat because he caught her smoking. He admitted that he really had done that. She also said she remembered him chasing her down the road in his truck while she was running with their baby in her arms. He often talked about going and kidnapping his other daughter.

He was always saying it should be the way it was a hundred years ago and that he wished he lived back then when people were 'real'.

When he was calm, I would confront him on the awful things he had said while he had been angry. He always assured me that he would never do any of the things he said; he would say he just had a problem with running his mouth when he was scared of losing me. He was usually caring and helpful over the next few weeks after behaving so poorly. That seemed to make it easy for me to overlook his bad behavior and forgive him.

Chapter 6
Going Back

A month after our daughter was born, I moved back in with him in Salt Lake with our baby girl and my boys. I believed, once again, that he would be better and we could work out the problems in our relationship.

It wasn't long after moving that I realized how unstable my situation was for my boys. Dusty was constantly telling me to leave, but of course he wouldn't really let me go. He just liked making me feel bad and enjoyed letting me know that I would have to leave without my daughter, which he knew I wouldn't do. I didn't want to have to suddenly take my older son out of school because we had to leave. He wanted to live with his dad, who was remarried and much more stable than I was at the time, and that helped me to be able to make the decision to let them go. My younger son didn't really understand, but I felt they should stay together. I didn't think it was fair that they should have to live with someone like Dusty. I wanted to leave him, but I felt like I was being pulled in a million directions. I was afraid of losing my daughter. I was afraid of what Dusty would do if I left him. More than anything, I just wanted to have a happy marriage and not put my kids through having any more divorced parents. A part of me hoped that everything would be okay someday and life would be normal. Unfortunately, I wouldn't know what life would bring from day to day, and I wasn't being fair to my boys by making them live that way with me. I asked Aaron if they could just come and stay with him for a few months until I could get my life more stable. He suggested letting them stay until the end of the school year, saying it would be better for them so they wouldn't have to change schools during the middle of the year. I reluctantly agreed, because it was so hard to let them go, but I trusted Aaron. I knew it was the right thing to do for them, but my heart ached. I was sick to myself for getting into that situation in the first place. He and his wife came and got them that very night. I think he was afraid I might change my mind if he waited. He said he was just going to have some legal papers drawn up saying he didn't have to pay child support while they were living with him.

I went camping with Dusty's grandma while he was gone driving truck the following week. He didn't want me to go camping because his cousin was going and he didn't like him. When I found out that Dusty's brother and his wife were going and his cousin's wife and kids were going, I figured it would be okay. Dusty's grandma even encouraged me to go and assured me it would be fun, so I fed the animals and we went. I left my car at the shop for Dusty so he'd be sure to have a way to get home from work when he got back from driving truck.

When I got home, he was fuming. He was angry because I went camping when he had told me not to. He said the lawn didn't get watered and he wanted me to be there when he got home. He said my priorities weren't straight. He complained that I was off having fun and letting everything else go. He called me names, threatened to 'beat my eyes shut', pushed me, and said he was leaving and taking our daughter with him. He kicked the fan across the room when I told him *his* priorities were the ones that weren't straight and that he was the one not taking care of things acting the way he did all the time. That was a *big* mistake on my part. After I said it, I had to do all I could to talk him out of hitting me. As he held me against the wall with his forearm against my throat, I begged him, I cried, I told him that he didn't want to do that. I tried to convince him that he *wouldn't* do such a thing! I would have said anything to make things better because he was scaring me so bad. He said he was going to the bar to 'have some fun'. I was glad! I hoped he would stay gone! He left, but came back twenty minutes later. He had only gone to the grocery store. When he returned, he had a new attitude and was 'so sorry' for his behavior. That night was one of the worst nights of my life up to that time. I had so much fear, mostly that he would take my daughter. I reached a point where I didn't care what he did to me, as long as he didn't take her. I hoped I would never have to feel that way again.

I didn't understand how he could say he was a secure person. He had to be the most insecure and angry person I had ever met.

He was driving truck long-haul for work at the time and usually traveled to the western states. His 2nd ex-wife lived in Oregon. I had never met her or talked with her. I wished I could have, just to get her take on things with Dusty. He told me she was a stripper and that he'd met her at a strip club while he was working as a bouncer. I had a hard time believing he was ever a bouncer because he wasn't exactly the type. The things he told me about her were rather hard to believe, especially coming from him. He was always comparing me to her and thought it would be great if I wanted to be a stripper too, he actually tried to encourage it, because 'they made a lot of money'. He told me she was severely abused as a child and had multiple personalities; he even described some of them to me. He said when she called him and told him she had filed for a common law marriage (they had lived together in Idaho for a year and a half), he told her to 'get to Salt Lake and be his wife then'. He said she was also bisexual and brought another girl with her for them to have a threesome with as a wedding gift to him. He tried to persuade me to consider doing the same. There was no way I would ever do such a thing. The very notion of it was extremely degrading to me, and from my point of view, it was cheating. He said during the two weeks she was there with him he was really cruel to her. He put her up against the wall in a chokehold and spit chewing tobacco in her face. He said he tried to rape her but wasn't able to, so he used something else to do it with. After that, she left him. I couldn't believe he told me all of that! I felt so sick. What purpose did it serve him if it was true, or if it wasn't true?

On one of his trips, he had to go through Oregon. He said he saw her walking into a store with another guy as he was driving through the town she lived in. I really had to wonder if he'd actually stopped to see her. He would never have told me if he had. He told me once toward the end of our relationship that she would call him about every three months to talk. I had no idea for the longest time; he'd hidden that well.

He tore his larynx (esophagus) tube around the 21st of August. I took him to the emergency room and did everything I could to help him and show him I cared, yet he still treated me like dirt. He was extremely demanding and I felt like his slave. I knew he was in pain, but so was I when I had been in labor; all he could do then was criticize me for wanting to have an epidural. I wasn't the only one that thought he was acting immature. The emergency room nurses even seemed to be annoyed with him.

The next day, while I was making a bottle for our baby girl, he demanded that I get him a drink right then. I wasn't happy with how he'd been treating me. He was standing right there at the sink getting ready to take his medicine and seemed to be trying to pick a fight with me. He was acting cocky and smug. I said, "Can't you get it? I'm making a bottle right now."

He knew he was getting on my nerves by the tone in my voice. He said, "You c---. What crawled up your c--- and died?" He was referring to the female anatomy. I couldn't believe he said that to me! How completely uncouth and disrespectful! I didn't cry. I just knew I couldn't tolerate that sort of treatment any longer.

Shortly after that, he came walking into the bathroom while I was doing my hair and wanted hugs and attention and was acting all grabby. I was so angry with him! I wanted him far away from me, and *not* touching me! He asked me what the matter was and asked why I was 'being so pissy and being a b---- -' to him. That was it! I'd had enough! I told him I couldn't believe he could act that way or talk to me that way, and yet say he cared about me and loved me. "That's just the way I am," he said matter-of-factly. I told him I was about ready to leave him. He said, "Fine, leave our daughter here though. She can go with me to L.A." I couldn't deal with him saying that. I would never leave without my baby girl and he knew it. If he really thought I was going to leave, he would take her with him on his trip driving truck, so I had to try to get along with him some more until I had an opportunity to get away.

Two days later, we had my boys and his other daughter visiting us. The three of them were sitting at the kitchen counter that morning eating breakfast. It also happened to be Dusty's birthday that day. Even so, I was frustrated with how he had been behaving toward me and didn't feel much like being around him. He walked in with his cocky attitude, and in front of the kids he asked me, "Why you being such a f------ c---to me?" Again, he was referring to the female anatomy. I was just completely speechless. He was impossible. I was more determined than ever to get the hell out of there!

That same day we had to tow my broken down car a few miles from where we were living. Dusty's mom came down to our house and watched the kids while we got the car. When we got back, she told Dusty that his ex-wife had called. Dusty yelled at his mother to not ever answer the phone when he wasn't home 'because his ex was a f------ c---'. He said this again in front of his other daughter and my two boys. His mom told me later that his daughter had started to cry and said he shouldn't call her mom names like that. She said he was mean and she hated him and sometimes wished he wasn't her dad. I couldn't say I blamed her.

That night, after Dusty left (driving truck to L.A.), I loaded up the truck with some of my bigger things. When I took the boys back to Aaron, I asked him if he would take those things to my parent's house since they both lived in the same town. I called my older brother and he was more than happy to come and get me and as much of my stuff as we could take back to his duplex. He lived about forty-five minutes away. They cleaned out a bedroom for me and my daughter to stay in. I felt really scared the first few days after I left. I was terrified that Dusty would find me and take my baby girl away. He told me he would blow his head off if I left him. I didn't believe him of course, but I was worried that he'd hurt me or someone around me. He said he would kill anyone that ever stood in his way of getting what he wanted. He said a lot of crap.

Letter to Dusty:

I cannot live with the insanity I constantly feel. You tell me I should take the boys and leave and we are just a pain to you. I cannot leave and not take my baby girl though. You can't use her as a threat to make me stay. You say you'll do these horrible things if I leave with her. Well I wouldn't keep her from you, but if you scare me with my life, I certainly will. If anything ever happens to me, I've got many family members and friends that care about me very much and would help me, and you would end up in prison or constantly hiding; either way it isn't freedom.

You act as though you could care less if my boys and I left. You say we are just in your way and keeping you from what you really want in life. We may have been the best thing for you. Your temper scares me. The things you say scare me. If you know they scare me and you still say them, then how can you truly say you care about me? I look back at all the letters you wrote me and at some of my journal entries. You loved me and were sorry all the time. 'Sorry' only becomes a word after a while. I hope you figure out that threatening me to get your way does not work. That isn't fair to me, Dusty. I'm not blaming everything on you. I'm not always easy to get along with and I make mistakes too. I don't feel, however, that I provoked you. I don't deserve to be called names, especially in front of my boys. They don't deserve to feel insecure or that we'll have to leave whenever there is an argument or disagreement. I don't deserve to have to worry about you hurting me or slashing my tires or taking precious things away from me when I don't see things your way. We are supposed to be a 'team'. That means we respect each other. It is not a one-sided deal where I do everything your way, or else. I have tried to do things your way and respect you but you still put me down. I don't want to wait until I get hit or you get hit or you decide to make me leave again without my baby. She is my baby too. I've only been here a month and how many times have you told me to leave? I didn't want to leave because I wanted this to work, but you've left me no choice.   Hanna

While I was at my brother's, I received the papers Aaron had drawn up that were supposed to only say he didn't have to pay child support while the boys lived with him. However, he also added that he would have primary custody until the school year was through, or until both parties mutually agreed it was in the best interest of the boys to be returned to me. If I didn't sign them, he would have taken me to court, for which I didn't have the money and he would have likely won, I thought. I didn't know hardly a thing about the law or how these things worked. I had no job, no income, no car, and was living with my brother. I imagined my case would have been weak. I felt betrayed by

Aaron, but he assured me that it was no big deal, so I trusted him and signed the papers. Shortly after the boys went to live with Aaron, he had a DNA test done to make sure my younger son was his. I told him several times before to go have a test done so he wouldn't have an excuse to hold something like that over me. I was glad he did it, but disgusted with him for his reasons. The next time we met with the boys, he said he'd gotten the results from the test, and then waited for my response. I just asked him if he was satisfied. Of course I knew what the results were, but in front of his wife, he had to say, "Don't act so high and mighty about it." I told him I certainly *would* act that way, and he knew exactly why.

It didn't take long for me to feel the heavy load of single parenting and feeling destitute. I had nothing and I felt helpless. I was extremely grateful to my brother for letting me stay in his home, but it was hard because I felt like I was a burden. I called Dusty a few weeks later. He was so happy to hear from me and was really nice. He begged me to come back. He promised he would change and do whatever he had to, to make our relationship work. He said he realized he had a problem and would get help. He said he would do all he had to do in order to help me get my boys back again. I believed him.

I moved back with him after only being gone a month. We were in the 'honeymoon phase' again and it seemed as though everything would be okay this time. Nonetheless, I got an ear-full about how much money it cost him each time I left. He and his brother worked on my car and he put some money into getting it fixed, but it only ran for a short time. He said we couldn't afford to live in that house anymore and that we would have to go stay with his grandma for a while. We moved in with her at the beginning of November. We didn't get along at all.

I'm vague on the details of a few incidents during this time, but I remember being on a high speed chase in Salt Lake, with him chasing after me. I couldn't believe there were no cops around to catch us when I needed them most! Another time, while we were at his grandma's, he wouldn't let me leave. He stood at the gate and wouldn't let me open it so I could drive my car through. His grandma's ranch was in the middle of some sand dunes where a lot of kids liked going and riding their motorcycles or four-wheelers around in. There were a lot of small hills and bike jumps scattered throughout the area. Going through the gate was the only road out of there. I backed my car up and drove over the hill into the sand dunes. I figured it would just have to do and hoped my car would handle it. Dusty ran after me and jumped up on the hood of my car and started hitting the windshield with his fist. He bent the windshield wipers and tried to break off my side mirror. He was screaming at me to stop and was making some pretty severe threats. I drove really fast and then slammed on the brakes to make him fall off, then drove away as fast as I could.

The following is taken from an actual police report I filed after another incident:

November 9th, Sunday

I woke Dusty up at 11 a.m. He asked how much money I had spent out of my checkbook. He didn't have his own checkbook. He refused to get one because then he could be tracked and didn't think it was anyone else's business how much money he had. I think he was worried that it would be garnished somehow for child support for his other daughter. I told him I had used enough to get enough gas to go pick up my boys (I had to meet their dad halfway) and that I bought the boys a Happy Meal at McDonald's. He asked, or should I say hollered "where is the rest of the cash?" I told him that I didn't cash his check; I only deposited it and used enough for gas to get my boys. He got really angry with me because he said I should have known he would need cash for the next day before he leaves (he drives truck long-haul). I told him that I did what he had asked me to do with it. After he got out of bed, he did nothing but holler at me and demand whatever it was he wanted. He was really ornery. I started ignoring him and told him I wasn't going to do things for him if he was going to act that way. He brought up things that he knew would make me angry and said really ignorant and hurtful things, including something derogatory about my son. I hated him for it and wanted him to stop talking to me! I tried to ignore

73

him. He kept it up. He sat down to fill out a form and asked me how to spell something that only had four letters. I sarcastically told him he should ask my 7-year-old son because he was asking a really dumb question and was just trying to get at me. He got mad and told me I could just get my boys and leave. Then he said "no, you have my money; we're going to go get it first". He had us all get in the car. I had already told him that the only way to get it all out would be to go to different stores and write a check for whatever amount they would allow because it was Sunday and the banks were all closed. I did not have an ATM card. He yelled the whole time and made rude comments about whatever he thought would upset me. He kept telling me how "f------stupid" I was for not getting any cash out for him. He slapped me upside the back of my head a couple of times as we were walking out to the car and stuck his thumb in my jaw (in a grip). I felt very scared. I really don't know what he'll do when he gets this way. I just wanted to stay calm because my boys were in the back seat. We went to Smith's in South Jordan first. Next we went to Albertson's in Riverton. He made comments about the girl walking out of the store and how good-looking she was to see if he could get me angry. I was angry but I wasn't going to let him know how much he was getting to me. We went to K-Mart in Sandy. When we were pulling out of K-Mart, he told me to get out of the car and take my boys with me. I figured that would be better than being in the car with him even though I didn't have any way to get anywhere, so I got out. Then he told me to get back in because he knew he couldn't get the rest of his money out of my checkbook without me. He told me how stupid I was and said he had had a girlfriend for the last month and a half and that I was too stupid to figure it out. I told him I didn't believe him. I knew he was just trying to anger me. He knew this would hurt me more than anything. My first husband had cheated me on many times before and this was a very tender spot. He told me who she was and the times he'd been with her in detail. He was holding me hostage in this car. I couldn't escape him. I begged him to let me and the kids out. He just kept talking and saying hurtful things. I knocked his cowboy hat off his head, grabbed his hair in the back, and punched him right in the jaw. He then punched me in the mouth and my head twice. He told me not to ever hit him. I just cried and told him I couldn't believe that he could do this to me. He said he was going to give me a black eye and then hit me in the eye and the nose. He hit my cheekbone and slapped me in the mouth with the back of his hand; that busted my lip open and it started to bleed. I told him my family was right about him, so he punched me in the jaw, which made me see stars. He drove and I cried. After a few minutes, he seemed to be calming down and started talking to my 7-year-old boy. I hated him talking to my son. I told him to please just let us go and to please just let me take the boys back to their dad (this was about 4:30 p.m.). I was supposed to meet the boy's dad at 7 p.m. (it was about a 1 hour and 45 minute drive). He said he didn't know what he was going to do and that he wasn't going to let me take the boys to their dad because their dad is a cop and didn't want him to see me or talk to me. Then he said, "Well you hit me first, what do I care?"

I said, "Dusty, you slapped me upside the back of my head and I didn't even hit you hard enough to leave any marks". He was holding me against my will in this car and would not let me go and take my kids. He was scaring me really bad. He was telling me the most hurtful thing he could think of and I had nowhere to go but to sit and listen to him. I think my hitting him was more like self-defense. I know it is not right to hit, but what would most people do in this situation? I had tried to make him stop the car. I had tried to get him to let me go. He got really mad again and said he was going to drop us off in the West Desert and let us walk because 'that would give him enough time to leave with our daughter'. I told him we'd hitchhike back and probably get picked up by some crazy guy that would do worse. I was hoping that he had some kind of heart and that he really didn't want to see worse harm come to us. I said, "I think we should just get these boys back to their dad." After a few minutes, he turned around (I think we were on Bingham Hwy). He said he was going to take me back to the house and beat me really bad. I told him that was fine, and then I'd throw him in jail.

He said, "You won't even be able to see or be recognizable when I'm through with you. Nobody will ever want you again." Then he said, "Maybe I will just lock you guys up somewhere in a room for a while so I can have enough time to leave with our daughter." He was almost to the house at this point. I was really afraid. Then he turned around because he said, "Grandma's home right now, I'll just wait until she leaves to go to church." I told him to just let me take the boys back to their dad. He pulled over to think about what he was going to do. He calmed down and told my older son that everything was okay and that he wasn't going to hurt him. My 4-year-old was asleep throughout most of this. He had fallen asleep almost as soon as we had gotten in the car. I was very glad for that. I told Dusty to just go back to the house so we could get the boy's bag and that I wouldn't let his grandma see me. I told him I would fix my make up and that he could go with me to take the boys back to their dad. He stopped at Maverik and bought the boys a candy bar and himself some chewing tobacco. While Dusty was in the store, I asked my older son if Dusty said anything to him while I was in the house getting their bags. He said that Dusty didn't want him to tell his dad about this. I told him to ignore whatever Dusty said and that he could tell his dad whatever he wanted to. Dusty took them to McDonald's and then we took them back to their dad.

Dusty has been by my side wanting to know everything and everyone I talk to. He told me to say he was giving me a piggyback ride and tripped over the dog and that I hit my nose on the back of his head. He has been trying real hard to be nice ever since. I think this will last about two to three weeks. *****

Earlier, when I had gone into Dusty's grandma's house where we were staying, she was there and she did see me. She knew I had been hit. My eye was red, I had been crying, and my lip was bleeding. She seemed a little concerned. As I was getting clothes out of the dryer, she came over to me and said, "Just don't receive it."

I asked her, "How do you not receive getting hit?" I told her that Dusty didn't want her to see me and to please not tell him that she did. I told her what he was going to say about what had happened and that it was a lie. I was crying and she seemed to have some empathy. I had to hurry and get the kid's bag because

I just wanted to get them out of there and back to their dad. I didn't like having them in the car waiting with Dusty either.

He had to go on a trip to Las Vegas shortly after this incident. I was angry with him and didn't want to be around him. I felt like I had to *act* like I wanted to be around him though, or I would suffer more consequences. He knew I wasn't happy, so he said he was going to go to Las Vegas and would be taking our daughter with him. I guess he figured that way he'd know I wouldn't be able to leave him. I couldn't have him take my daughter without me. She was five months old and I was her primary caretaker. She needed me. Dusty didn't have the patience to take care of her, especially while he was driving and working. I told him I would go with him too. I knew that I either had to go or he would take her without me. That trip gave him time to try to convince me of all the reasons why he acted the way he did and to try and make it up to me. Each time we stopped at a truck stop, I felt like I must look like some kind of prostitute or something getting out of the semi with a black eye. The makeup I bought to cover it didn't work well. I felt sad. I think Dusty felt pretty bad about what he did. It seemed to pain him to look at my face he'd beaten. I hoped it ate his conscience. When we got back from the trip, I felt confused, scared, trapped, and angry. I just acted like everything would be okay. I had to, until I knew how to get out. I felt like I lived in a prison with him and his grandma. He had to go on another trip about a week later. I figured that would have to be my opportunity to leave.

On November 20th, I didn't feel like doing much of anything. I felt really depressed. Still, Dusty's grandma required that we each do ten hours of work per week because it was part of living at the ministry ranch. I was supposed to help her do some deep cleaning in the living room that day. We started talking in the living room and she told me I was 'affecting the ranch by moping around, not doing anything, and being depressed'. I told her that I was upset because of what had happened. She was so cold to me. She said, "Well you're not dead; you're not going to die from it." Yeah, I thought, not this time anyway. I couldn't believe her! It didn't matter to her what happened to me. All she seemed to care about was Dusty and what *he* wanted. She wanted us to stay together and she wanted me to do everything Dusty asked me to do and to be a good wife. One time, after having a lot of problems with him, we were all upstairs in the living room and I was getting ready to walk downstairs when Dusty asked me what I was doing. I didn't know if that question was meant for the next day or right then, but I was so upset with him that I just told him it was none of his business, kind of snotty-like. His grandma heard me say this to him. She brought it up later and said it was pretty horrible that I would talk to him that way. It was no wonder to her that Dusty was mean to me. I think she figured I probably deserved it. She had no idea what had been going on previously.

I was planning on leaving that day. I talked to my friend, Nicole, on the phone during the week and told her what had happened. Somewhere in the back of my mind, I thought if I died, I wanted someone to know what had been going on and not let Dusty lie his way out of it. She told me I needed to leave and that she would help me. She gave me a lot of good advice.

I was downstairs getting my hair done and getting ready to leave when Dusty's grandma came down and informed me that since he was gone driving truck, I needed to do his ten hours of work too. I just said, "I see." I think that made her mad. She mimicked me with an "I see" and walked off. I guess she figured she would work the depression out of me.

I went outside to leave but she caught me on my way out. I was hoping to leave without her knowing, but she was already outside. She came running over and asked me where I was going. I told her I just needed to go to the store. She asked what for. I named off a few things but she didn't seem happy about it. I really felt like she was my curator sometimes. She was probably worrying for Dusty that I would leave him. She said we needed to clean the living room at 1:00 that day. I had to take her car, the Lincoln, which Dusty and I used for transportation at the time. I was afraid she wouldn't let me go because it was 'her car' but she didn't dispute it too much. I left and went straight to the police station where I had them take a picture of my bruises and wrote a report (the one included previously in this book). I was grateful it didn't cost anything to file a police report or to get a protective order. They were nice to me there. I called Nicole, and asked her if she would come and get me from the police station when I got back from getting my stuff. I was going to take a policeman back to the ranch to get my things and then leave Dusty's grandma's car there. Boy was his grandma mad! She wanted the police off her property and was making comments about me leaving. I was almost afraid of how she would have acted when I got there if I didn't have some people with me. I packed as much into the cop car as I was able to and as fast as I could.

I went back to the cop station and Nicole picked me up from there and took me to her house in the Avenues. I called my parents and they came and picked me up the next day. I could tell my dad was nervous to look at my face for the first time in seeing me after the incident, but he was okay. I was just glad that almost two weeks had gone by since it had happened. My black eye was almost gone. I'm sure he didn't know quite what to expect. I went home with them and stayed with them for the next month and a half.

I was really worried about how Dusty was going to react when he got back from his trip to find the police there waiting to arrest him. I knew he would be furious. I called the police station and asked them how it went. They said he was really upset and yelled a lot and said that I had started it. I had to laugh out loud. It sounded like a four-year-old that got caught and threw a fit about it. He called his dad to come and bail him out, which his dad did. His dad paid $1000. I don't know if that was bail money or for an attorney. He was only in jail for a couple of hours. I wished his family would stop enabling him, but he was really good at convincing others of his innocence and making them feel sorry for him.

I lost a lot of weight. That is what I usually did when I was stressed. I had lost a lot of weight when I was separated from my first husband. During that separation I weighed 105 lbs. I weighed 136 lbs. at full term with my second son, which was relatively inadequate at 5'7". I weighed about 112 lbs. this time.

Dusty started calling my parent's house all the time. I somehow felt compelled to talk to him. I felt bad that he had gone to jail. I felt bad that he was so upset and that he missed me so much. I agreed to see him when he came through town on a trip driving truck. I was starting to feel the symptoms of another pregnancy, so I took a test in the bathroom at a restaurant when he came through town. It looked negative and I felt relieved! I had just had a baby five months before, and getting pregnant again so soon was the last thing I wanted, especially under the circumstances! We walked out to the car and Dusty was getting into his truck when I threw the test in the back of his truck into a box. Just as I was leaving, Dusty got out and looked at the test again and stopped me. He said it was *positive*. I looked at it. It really was. I was numb. *He* was excited though. To him, this probably meant he would get me back again. I had a lot of mixed feelings.

I continued to talk to Dusty on the phone and he agreed to do counseling before it was actually court ordered. Why did I give in when he convinced me to believe him again? Why did I let my loneliness have such power over me? Why did I do such stupid things?

I moved back to Salt Lake into an apartment (in Dusty's name once again, but only because he promised he would help me get on my feet even if I didn't want to be with him) and went back to college again. I agreed to go with him to his counseling each Saturday. I felt I should still try since I was pregnant again. Dusty agreed to help me by letting me drive his truck to school and by watching our daughter when he could. His other grandma said she would tend sometimes too. It was so hard not having my own car! It still wasn't in working condition and I didn't have the money to get it fixed. I wanted to try to find a job but I didn't know how to do it while going to school full time and trying to find a daycare, all without a vehicle and being pregnant, and not to mention my unstable relationship. I didn't have a phone because I needed to pay my previous bill before I could get it hooked up. I didn't know how I was going to pay rent by February 1. Dusty would say he didn't want me to work because 'my child support would go up'. I thought that was ridiculous and refused to run from it like he always did. Later on, he would complain that I *needed* to work and that *he* was the only one doing anything. His opinion on the matter seemed to depend on the day, how he was feeling at the moment, and what worked best for him.

One night, Dusty showed up at my apartment and said his grandma kicked him out of her house. I was quite upset about this and he knew it. I knew she felt like living with me was what he should be doing, but I still wondered if she had actually made him leave. He went on to say it was *my* problem if I didn't want him there and that I would either have to live with him or go live somewhere else. He knew I had no other options at the time. He told me how ungrateful I was being. I wanted to continue the counseling and have things get better before we lived together again! I wanted my boys to be able to come visit me without him there! I wanted to feel safe and have my own refuge! I felt like such a failure in my attempt to do things right.

He didn't care about my opinion anymore and he didn't seem to care if I got to have my boys. He said it was my fault to begin with for having them gone. He said it was my fault that he got angry and blew up, and my fault he hit me.

He started to complain constantly about the gas I had to use when I took his truck to school.

What good did it do to go to counseling with him if we had to sit there and lie? He would let me know what I was allowed to tell her before each appointment. She told us first thing upfront that we should *not* live together or spend hours upon end with each other. Well, Dusty lived with me and spent hours with me, but I couldn't tell her that because 'then the courts would know'. It seemed the real reason he went to begin with was because he was expected to legally. He went on to say that counseling should be last priority because it cost money. He would say that he and our money should come first.

He wanted me to do everything for him at the apartment, I guess to help me see that he really was first and foremost. My schooling and I were no longer priorities to him. His truck and his job came first. He called me names and would tell me to just leave if I said anything he didn't like or if I acted upset about our living conditions. Aside from him being there, I was quite uncomfortable without any furniture. I was pregnant and had to sleep on the floor.

I really needed God on my side, but that was someone else for him to try and keep from me. He had no respect for my belief in God. He would say he didn't believe in Him. He would frequently put down me, my religion, my beliefs, my family, and anything that had to do with God. However, he would tell me it would be okay if I wanted to be a 'real witch' and actually practice witchcraft. He thought that would be more interesting and tried to encourage it. He considered it to be just fine to drink, smoke, chew, hate people, fight, and swear. Though I don't think it makes a person bad if they choose to do the first three of those things, unless of course the drinking is causing problems, we obviously had different ideas about what we would teach our kids.

I felt let down. I was quite unhappy and told him how upset I was about everything. He told me to leave and that I'd better be gone before he got back from work the next morning or he'd call the police and have me thrown out. He was extremely angry when he told me this and was acting violent and shouting right in my face. I thought he might actually hurt me. He pushed me halfway off the chair I was sitting on and held me down while he told me to leave. I called Nicole as soon as he left and she came and got me. I stayed with her for a week, and then with my cousin for almost two weeks, so I could finish out the school semester.

Of course Dusty said he didn't mean any of the things he had said. He said he didn't think I would actually believe him and leave. He was 'so sorry' and wanted me to 'please come back'. More tears, more pleading, blah, blah, blah. He bought me a dozen roses and brought them to me at my school. I dropped them in the trash can. They didn't mean a thing to me. I started hating roses. He gave me some money for some formula and food too, but I would not go back to him.

I felt sad, relieved, and scared after breaking up with him; sad, because I thought I loved him and because he had been trying harder in a lot of ways; relieved, because I hated him for being so awful at times. He could be *really* mean and terrifying when he was mad. I felt scared because I didn't know how I would be able to start over again. I wanted to move back to where my boys lived because my heart ached for them so much. I had some family and friends there. There were a few disadvantages; however, the advantages outweighed the bad. I had to figure out how I would move my stuff, how to get an apartment and car, get registered for school, find a daycare, a doctor, a job, and how I would get my bills paid. It seemed so overwhelming. That's partly why it was always so difficult to leave. Starting over was quite a challenge, especially with a baby and being pregnant.

Why couldn't Dusty understand why it was hard for me to find work? He always thought I was just coming up with excuses. I didn't want to work in Salt Lake because I wanted to be anywhere but there. Nobody wanted to hire a pregnant woman close to delivering. I tried doing daycare at home so I wouldn't have to pay for daycare myself and so I could be with the kids. Our relationship was so rocky though, I couldn't be sure what each day would bring and having other kids there was unwise. I worked at my brother's house on the computer doing some editing, but I didn't make hardly anything doing that. I worked for a temp service for a while, but Dusty and I didn't stay together and I always had to be the one to leave. When I was back in Salt Lake again, Dusty didn't want me to work because he was afraid Aaron would raise my child support and he didn't feel we could afford it, but I don't think that was the real reason. Working gave me independence and friends. When I went to school full time, I couldn't find work to accommodate my school schedule and be during the open daycare hours. I had to ask my family to babysit my daughter and for rides to and from school. I was sure nobody enjoyed that. To take me to and from work on top of that seemed like a joke. Why did I even bother with school? It was a burden on everyone who had to haul me around. Welfare was out of the question. Dusty would threaten me a lot and put me down for even thinking about getting help in that way.

I lived with my younger brother and my sister-in-law for a couple of months. I basically stayed in my room with my daughter and kept to myself. I didn't want to be a burden on anyone. My sister-in-law was great; she coerced me out of there and told me to be a part of the family. I was so grateful for her. She helped me come out of my shell a little bit and realize that I could 'tell Dusty to kiss my a--'. That language came easy for her and didn't for me at the time. It was kind of a good feeling to say that out loud. It was empowering.

Dusty had my car fixed and brought it to me, which I was really happy about. I was so grateful I didn't have to ask for rides from everyone. He wanted to get back together, but I wasn't about to move again. One day, when I was leaving job service, he pulled into the parking lot to talk to me. He was in his truck and I remember him getting upset with me because I refused to get back together with him. He threatened to leave and said I'd never see him again, to which I was actually quite happy about! I told him to go on and leave then. He was rather hurt by my cold, non-caring attitude. I proceeded to drive away anyway. He followed me and kept yelling that he wanted to talk and was getting pretty angry. I just kept driving. He tried to run me off the road and when I came to the stop light, he pulled his truck up and around to the front of my car so I couldn't go forward. He jumped out of his truck and ran up to my window yelling at me to pull over. Luckily, there was a cop sitting at the corner watching the whole thing and immediately pulled us both over. Dusty suddenly had a change of attitude and started begging me to let him talk to me. He even started crying to the officer. He pulled out some cash and asked the officer to please give it to me. I took it, shaking my head at his fake pleas.

I finally got an apartment through some housing assistance. It was a nice place and the management kept it maintained well. When I lived there, my caseworker told me not to work until after I had my baby. It was hard to know what to do. Without some schooling to help me get a better job, it seemed impossible to find something that would pay my bills and daycare for two babies.

I started taking anti-depressants in May. That wasn't easy for me. I wasn't sure how much they worked and Dusty would always criticize me for taking them. He insisted that I not *ever* take them in front of our kids. He didn't want them to think you just take a pill to solve all your problems. Even so, I knew they helped me somehow and I didn't know of any other alternatives.

Dusty moved to a nearby ranch to be closer to where I lived. I told him I was not leaving my apartment to go back to him. It was too hard to start over and move everything, and I was pregnant. I didn't want to lose what I had going. I was actually making some progress. I told him *he* could be the one to move and start over for a change. He would come and visit sometimes and was mostly nice. As long as we were getting along, it became very easy to forget about why we weren't together in the first place.

As time went on, he kept making hints about getting married. I didn't want to – it scared me, but I wanted my baby to be born in wedlock, I wanted things to work out, and I wanted a whole family. I kept thinking it would be that way someday. Finally, in July, he said that we were either getting married that day in the court or he was leaving for good. Romantic, huh? We got married. My family was shocked but they still tried to accept him.

I asked my doctor if he'd induce my labor on Dusty's birthday if I hadn't given birth yet. I was already dilated quite a bit the week before and the doc couldn't figure out why I hadn't had my baby by then. He ended up inducing my labor on Dusty's birthday. I had my fourth child, a son, five hours later. Dusty was acting extremely childish and selfish while I was in the hospital. He said I was being such a wimp for having an epidural and he was mad at me for that. He was acting like he had to control everything. I really didn't know what his problem was. I had the name and spelling picked out for our son months before and he had been okay with it then, but he decided to change the spelling that day. He wouldn't let me put the birth announcement in the paper. He didn't want our son circumcised, but I had that done regardless. He wouldn't let me give our baby a pacifier. He just wanted the opposite of anything I wanted. I finally just started crying and couldn't stop. He got really mad about that and told me to quit acting like a baby. I'd just *had* a baby and he was acting like a total jerk to me. The nurse saw me crying and told the doctor. They asked Dusty to leave so I could get some rest. He went home and said he was taking our daughter and that I'd have to figure out how I was getting home on my own. He went on to say that he couldn't believe I was acting like such a 'b----' and making a big scene by crying. I had tried not to cry. Of all the times to be so cruel, to say such hurtful things, and to act so selfish! I was really glad he left! When my doctor came in to check on me, I was crying uncontrollably. They put me in a different room in another area of the hospital. It was much quieter and I didn't have to share it with someone else. The doctor gave me something to help me sleep and said I really needed to get some rest. The nurses took care of my baby that night. Dusty never said he was sorry. He never thought he had acted badly.

He quit his job at the ranch a couple of weeks later because he said he didn't get along with all the young guys. He said all they wanted to do was drink. He never did have any close friends. My guess was that they probably couldn't stand him after a while because he would never stop talking. He 'knew everything' and 'had already done everything ten times better than anyone else'.

He started working at a mine in Nevada at the end of the summer. He lived there in a camp trailer for a couple of months because I wanted to wait to move until after I was healed up and more settled with our new baby. I moved into a house with him that October.

Chapter 7

From Bad to Worse

Dusty was quite hard on me from the time I got there. He was constantly telling me I was slow, lazy, ungrateful, and that I didn't do s---. Just because I wasn't earning money, his outlook on the matter was that I wasn't helping or doing anything. Of course, I was taking care of two babies, three counting Dusty, but sometimes I thought he should count for three all by himself. I couldn't find a job that paid enough to make it slightly worth the effort after paying daycare expenses for two babies, buying formula instead of breastfeeding, and the expense of a second vehicle. It was simply cheaper for me to stay at home and better for the babies. I tried really hard to be economical with the food. I made everything I could from scratch including bread, chili, stew, chicken noodle soup, granola, biscuits, pie, turkey, brownies, salads, and much more. I had to cook everything perfect or Dusty, my big spoiled brat, wouldn't eat it and he'd complain like crazy. This is what I would constantly hear from him:

"Do as you're told!

Do it now!

You don't work a quarter as hard as I do.

I'll quit being an a--hole when you earn it.

I'll give you respect when you do as you're told and start earning it.

I work my a-- off.

I want food. I want it the way I like it!

I want it quiet!

If you'd shut your mouth and do as you're told, we would get along.

Shut him (our baby boy) up!

Get her (our toddler daughter) now!

I'm starving to death!

I'm sick.

I'm tired.

I work, so I can act that way.

A real wife would....

*You're never gonna be a rancher's wife being slow and dumb;
use your head.*

Why can't you be more like my grandma?

I will disable your car if you try to leave (which he did).

You can leave if you don't like it, but you're not taking the kids.

I'll kill you if you take the kids.

I will hunt you down and you'll wish you hadn't taken the kids.

*You worthless f------, wh---, c---, b----, just leave! You don't do
anything I ask, so just leave."*

*(He considered abuse to be only when the guy beats up the
woman daily, therefore he was not abusive).*

He was always telling me to leave but said I better never take the kids or he would kill me. I kept a small Ziploc baggie with money and an extra key to my car outside in a hiding place in case of an emergency. He was in control of all the money and made sure I never had any in my possession without him knowing exactly what I had spent it on. He always wanted to see the receipts to make sure.

I tried my hardest to do everything he asked. I was constantly trying to please him. He only made me hate him. Why would I have any desire to be what he wanted me to be when he acted like that? Yes, I talked back. I didn't want to be a puppet! Yet, I did feel like a puppet. I hoped he would stop. I hoped when

I started earning money he would stop. That seemed to be what it was all about.

Letter to Dusty:

I'm filled with so much pain and hurt it makes my stomach wrench. I can't eat. My heart actually burns with pain and I just shake and I cry and the tears just keep coming and they won't stop. Why? You're hurting me. Do you hear me? You're HURTING me. I'm trying to tell you something. Will you listen to me? I try to please you. I try to be strong. Nothing I do is right by you. Nothing is ever good enough. You are always so disappointed in me. I'm really trying – do you hear me? I pray for you and for us. I don't want it to end. I will never leave again if you will please stop hurting me. It's killing me. Do you care? Please have a heart and care. I need your praise and your encouragement, not your constant criticism. I need you to be understanding and kind. Please be patient with me. You're breaking me down and it hurts so much. Don't break my spirit. Please just love me and understand me. I'm your friend, not your enemy. Please hear what I'm telling you and open your heart to me. Do you understand what I am saying? Please, please try. Try for us and this family. Please see the good in me. I do some things right, don't I? I am not trying to hurt you so please just accept me. Don't speak as if there could ever be another. That hurts me deeply. Whether you think I shouldn't feel that way or not, when you make little comments like that, it really torments me. Don't you understand that I can't change that feeling? Do you love me enough that you could be considerate of my feelings even if you don't agree? Do I matter to you at all? Please remember that the things you say mean so much to me. I love you. I'm begging you to please try to accept me and love me for who I am. I don't like to fight. I don't like to hurt. Please be my friend, my true friend, and my true love.

Love,

Hanna

(I know, insert PATHETIC here, ha ha).

We went grocery shopping at the store thirty miles away from our home one night in November. Dusty had been so rude to me throughout the whole shopping trip. He was giving me the "I work my a-- off and you don't deserve sh--" talk. On the way home, he asked me to shift gears while he was eating his fried chicken. I was sitting next to him in the middle of the cab. I hated to shift the gears for him while he was driving because I couldn't ever find the right one. He would act like I was so stupid when I couldn't find it. He knew I didn't like to shift the gears and he also knew I wasn't happy with the way he was acting. I told him to shift it. He yelled at me, slammed on the brakes, which made the groceries all slide to the front of the truck, and then he threw his chicken at the far window just passing by my face. He opened his door and jumped out and then told me to get out and walk home. I said 'no' and just ignored him. It was freezing outside! He got back in the truck and verbally abused me all the way home. I hated him when he did that. Whenever he acted like that and then settled down, he would want me to be an all-loving wife and act like nothing was ever wrong. I hated him. I wished he was gone. I wished he would just die!

November 27

About a week later, Dusty came home from work a bit early and was in a really bad mood. He came home at 7:55 p.m. He usually got home between 8 and 8:30 pm. I was in the kitchen cooking him dinner. He got really mad because it wasn't ready for him the moment he walked in and he had to wait twenty minutes for his dinner. I was making him a nice dinner with steak, salad, baked potatoes, and steamed vegetables. He got mad again because he said I was cooking the steak wrong. He kept demanding things and yelling about anything he could think of. He was yelling things like 'I hate baked potatoes; you're cooking the steak wrong; give me the fork; turn it down now; that's not enough flour…whoa, that's enough'. I told him to cook the damn steak himself and pushed the frying pan to a different burner. He said, "Don't get pissy with me or I'll throw this hot oil in your face!" The first steak almost burned. He told me I had to eat it because we weren't going to waste it and I had already ruined it for him. He cooked his steak and I left the kitchen to feed the baby. He yelled at me to get back in there and finish dishing up his plate and to finish cooking the steak I ruined because I was going to eat it.

I couldn't understand why he felt the need to act this badly or what gave him the right to treat me this way. I was in tears. I knew this situation would only get worse if I didn't do what he wanted. I went in and dished up his salad and vegetables. I asked him if he wanted sour cream on his potato. He grabbed the potato and threw it in the sink so hard that there was nothing left of it. He said, "That's what I think of your f------ potato! I told you I hate baked potatoes!" He went in the living room with his steak. I poured him some water and took it and his salad and vegetables to him in the living room. He saw the tears, but he didn't care.

He said he hated me because I destroyed his whole life. He said I ruined all his dreams and had done nothing but cost him money. He'd done nothing but cause me grief! I wouldn't have 'cost him so much' if he would have stopped making me leave all the time and stopped hurting me. He would say the kids were costing him and that he wished he'd never met me then he wouldn't have any of these 'problems'.

He told me to leave, again, though he would never actually let me go. He was always saying things like, 'I wish you would leave with the kids so I'd have an excuse to kill you. I'd have nothing to lose'. He would say he wanted to go to hell, that he didn't believe in God, and that his life was already hell because he wasn't living on a ranch riding horses. He sat and told me this that night and also added that I was a worthless c--- (female anatomy) who ought to be shot. I told him I wouldn't leave without my kids and that I didn't want to die, so I was staying. He said, 'you'd better not leave because I will kill you if you do, and if you ever get a boyfriend, I'll cut his head off and shove it up your c--- (female anatomy) until you bleed to death'. He went on to say some other appalling things along the same lines. He was so crazy. I didn't believe anything he was saying; he was always saying the most alarming things to sound tough and to scare me. It did scare me; it scared me that anyone would even talk that way and think it was okay.

That night he pushed me into the kid's little wooden picnic table and it left a big bruise on the back of my leg. He knocked the lamp over and it hit my daughter in the head, but it didn't hurt her. He kicked the coffee table up on me with his plate of steak and salad and vegetables. I got salad all over me and the coffee table left a bruise on my shin. My baby boy was in my lap and my daughter was sitting next to me when this happened. Dusty yelled right in my face really loud and it startled my baby; he was only three months old. I was crying really hard and begged him to stop acting this way. He punched a glass-framed picture in the hall. I could never keep any framed pictures hanging up for long. He always broke them, unless it was his. He threw his plate with the steak across the room and it shattered against the wall by the wood stove. Then he threw the picture I had of me and the kids onto the floor and spit on it, which ruined it. I was trying to tune him out and ignore him by staring at the television. I didn't want to give him any attention for his bad behavior and I also felt petrified and didn't know what else to do but sit still with the kids. He picked up the wood cutting ax, which really freaked me out, and then threatened to break the television if I didn't start paying attention to him. He threatened to tear up my pictures, including the ultrasound picture of our baby. I begged him to stop. I was really terrified! He told me I'd better leave or he was going to kill me. I knew he wouldn't let me go however, especially with the kids. I told him I couldn't leave without them.

I always thought that he was going to do better when he'd beg me to come back and make all kinds of promises. He would constantly call me on the phone and try to keep me on for hours at a time. He'd write me letters and poems and cards telling me how much he loved and cared about me. I always ended up feeling let down after going back and deeply regretting my decisions. Each time after I'd come back and a short period of time had passed, he would tell me again that I had ruined his life.

Now, I *couldn't* leave anymore. I married him. My family was probably ready to disown me. I had nowhere to go, no money, no nothing. I would have to ask myself how long I could continue to do this. I dreaded the consequences if I couldn't make it work. He wanted me to be perfect but there was no perfect. He was doing nothing but turning me against him in his efforts to 'train me'.

It's funny; on the outside we looked like such a happy little young family. We even got compliments on how 'cute' our family was. Dusty could be so polite and sweet when we were around other people, but he could be such a monster when we were alone.

After a while, he started to settle down. I wasn't as scared anymore and felt safe enough that I could talk to him about how I felt. I told him he was abusive and that I couldn't live this way. I asked him if he wanted his kids to grow up seeing this all the time and said that my boys were not with me because of this type of behavior. He started feeling really bad for himself; he cried and told me he was very sorry. I think he realized how badly he'd acted and was afraid I was going to leave. I hugged him and told him I wasn't leaving but he really scared me when he acted like that. I told him I would not leave based on my 'current emotions' but if he continued to scare me, I could not stay. He was always telling me I was too emotional and shouldn't act on 'feelings'. What was I *thinking?*

Nov 28

Dusty came home early from work the next day because he was sick with worry that I'd leave. I told him to get some sleep and that I wasn't leaving. We got along good until that night. I had been fairly upset most of the day because of the events from the day before and hadn't felt like doing too much. Although I did do some work, it probably didn't look like much because they were things you wouldn't really notice. I dusted the ceiling fan, washed the light fixtures, did some laundry, vacuumed, cleaned around the stove (I had to clean up the steak and broken plate), dusted shelves, did dishes, and sorted photos. I still had my photos scattered all over the table when he got up because I wasn't finished sorting through them. He proceeded to run his finger along the top of the doors, and yes, they were covered in dust. I never dusted there. I hadn't raked the leaves in the yard like he wanted either. All we had was a mulching rake. I tried to rake with it but it really made my back hurt. I wasn't about to rake all one and a half acres that way. Dusty said he figured I'd find an excuse for not doing it. He spit water in my face and I got another lecture of how I didn't do anything.

December 4

Dusty could be a real sweetheart when he wanted to be. It was the times in between incidents when I enjoyed being with him and life felt okay. He would laugh and play and say sweet things. Why did he have to be so cruel sometimes?

He burned all of my diaries. I had to sit and watch as he threw each one of them into the wood burning stove. I wouldn't let him find any more in the future. He felt threatened and jealous by them. He didn't think I should be keeping my diary from high school because it talked about a couple of guys I dated, and my other diaries were from when I was married to Aaron. Dusty was always accusing me of still being in love with Aaron. I wasn't. I wished Dusty would grow up. I wished he would stop tormenting me. I spent a lot of time wishing.

December 24

Dusty was upset with me and said I was being ungrateful about the Christmas gifts he'd helped me buy. He had spent thirty-five dollars on each of the boys and about seventy-five dollars on each of our babies. The boys were visiting for the holiday and I wanted Christmas to be fun. I was wrapping their presents when he told me I could wrap the baby's presents but not my boy's because *he* bought them and he wasn't responsible for them, I was. He said we were going to take their gifts back to the store. I kept wrapping them anyway, slowly, because I wasn't sure what he would do and hoped and prayed my boys could not hear him talking. I hated him more than ever. Christmas morning was not cheery. We were running behind and he wanted to go to Salt Lake that day. His ex-wife was going to bring his daughter over to his dad's that day and he didn't want to be late. I had to pack all four kid's bags, clean up all the Christmas stuff and get everyone fed and ready. He yelled at me and put me down the whole way there because he was afraid I had made him late. It was about a three and a half hour trip. When we got there, he told me to 'put a smile on my face and act happy so I didn't ruin Christmas any more than I already had'. It turned out we weren't that late and his other daughter hadn't showed up yet.

Jan 12

I had been pretty upset with Aaron over the previous two weeks since hearing that when he would talk about our boy's 'mom', he meant their stepmom, and when he talked to them about me, he would just say 'Hanna' because it was 'less confusing'. I thought that was wrong to refer to me as *Hanna* and not their *mother*! I finally called him and said, "Aaron, I have a problem and I need you to just listen to me without saying anything for a minute." I told him that I didn't think it was right to refer to me as 'Hanna' to our boys. I told him my parents didn't like each other much but always referred to the other parent as "your mom" or "your dad". I told him I considered it to be disrespectful and the boys needed to know I am their mother. I told him it hurt me very much that he would do that and I started to cry. He was really nice and said he didn't realize it would upset me so bad and that they really hadn't done it that much. Dusty came in and was listening to my phone conversation, as he always did, and was getting quite upset with me. He was standing there in the background telling me to 'grow up and stand up for myself' and 'stop kissing Aaron's a--' all while I was on the phone trying to have a conversation. He got really mad when I started crying! I honestly couldn't see how I was doing anything wrong. I felt hurt and I couldn't help but cry when letting Aaron know how upset I was. He was being nice about the whole thing, so why should I be rude? I asked to talk to my younger son for a minute so Dusty would give me a break, and I really hoped Aaron couldn't hear what Dusty was saying. When I hung up, Dusty lit into me. He said we were through and that it all ended with us after that phone call. How insane could he be? I didn't know what I had done so wrong. He made some derogatory comment about me and Aaron and added that I was 'kissing his a-- bawling to him like that'. I told Dusty he needed to grow up! He pushed me into the hall and from then on for the next two and a half hours, he called me the most awful names. I still didn't feel like I had done anything wrong. All I could think about was how Dusty needed to grow up and get over his insane insecurities, but then I would question myself, and start to wonder if I actually *had* done something wrong. Sometimes he really confused me.

He pushed me against the wall and I pushed him back away from me. After all, hadn't he just gotten done telling me how I needed to stand up for myself? Again, he yelled the same derogatory comment about me and Aaron, so I screamed and kicked at him to keep him away from me. I just wanted him to leave me alone! In this fight, I yelled back my disapproval of all the things he kept saying. I hated being treated this way and I was sick of it! I didn't care if he beat me up or said mean things. I refused to cower to him this time. My respect for him was ZERO. He kept telling me to leave and asked if he 'could make that any more clear'. He said he didn't care where I went or how I got there; I would be walking, of course, and wouldn't be taking the kids. I was *really* upset because Dusty was sitting there with the phone in his hand saying he was going to call my dad to 'come get his daughter' and was telling me that we were done and if I wanted to 'kiss Aaron's a--' then I should just go back to him. I was furious. I was so tired of him telling me to leave with nothing and telling me I had better leave or he was going to kill me. I was tired of him *not* letting me leave after telling me I had to. I was tired of being held hostage in my own home. I was tired of his threats and his stupid insecurities. I was more afraid than anything of not having my babies with me when I left. I just couldn't do that. I would never leave without them. I pushed the television tray over onto the floor, which broke the glass and bowl that was sitting on it. The bowl had some soup in it that Dusty had spit in earlier because 'that wasn't what he wanted for dinner'. He took the gold buckle and leather belt that he'd bought for me for Christmas and yelled, "This cost me eighty bucks and you don't deserve it!" He always took back any gifts he had 'given' me, including my gold wedding band, which he took the pliers to and made into a little ball once when he was upset with me. I never let myself get attached to any material things for that reason. He took the kid's shot records and social security cards and said he would always find me no matter what. He said if I tried to contact him or his family or if I ever got on welfare and ruined his life financially, that he would find me and kill me. He went on to tell me I was white trash and that I couldn't make it financially without him. He said me and his ex-wife would both be raising his kids as 'white trash pieces of sh--'. All I could think was, '*News flash for you Dusty, when you treat women like this, guess what it makes you*?!' He would then tell me I would never get the kids and that he would find an attorney like the one he'd dated before me, move in with her, and spend every dime he had until he had full custody of the kids.

I had to wonder why he would want them so bad when he was always saying he wished he had never had kids. Earlier that same evening he was saying the most horrible things about that very subject. Up to that point in time, he still hadn't changed a single diaper. He was always complaining to me to "get him!" if our baby boy was fussing. He would say terrible things because he was extremely immature and couldn't handle crying kids. One night when our son woke up crying, Dusty snarled, "I'll shut that little son of a b---- up!" and proceeded to jump out of bed. I pushed him right back down and firmly told him he certainly would not! I slept in the living room with the baby for a week after that. He said other unbelievable things that I wouldn't even repeat. They were along the lines of 'he wanted a boy, not a boob' and how we should get rid of him and start over. How could he say such things? He would always say he never really meant it, that he just ran his mouth when he was mad. Why would he even *say* those things like he's half crazy then? I didn't trust him alone with our son and made sure that didn't happen. He didn't act like that to our daughter though, because 'she's a girl'. He told me he was so upset that he'd met me and had kids because it ruined his life and now he couldn't be a champion like he should have been. I told him to go and be a stupid 'champion' but not to forget what it cost him.

I was sitting on the couch holding my baby boy on my lap and Dusty was walking around still yelling at me and calling me names and saying the most unspeakable things. He told me he hated me and wished I was dead. I felt that way about him too, but I would never say it. He said he hoped I would do him and the kids a favor and commit suicide. He told me I deserved to die, and if it weren't for the law, he'd shoot me right then. He said he should take his gun and shove it up my c--- (female anatomy) and pull the trigger. Then he went in the bedroom and got his gun. He came out and yelled, "Where's my bullets, b----?!" I told him I didn't know, of course! He then said, "I'm not gonna shoot you, where's my bullets? My guns are going with me. If you try to have the cops come, then I will shoot them! I hope you have the cops come. I dare you!"

He knocked everything off the dresser and found his bullets. It was almost getting to be time for him to go to work, so he tried to be a little nicer. I still didn't feel like I had done anything wrong in my conversation with Aaron, but Dusty kept insisting that I owed him an apology. Yes, I thought to myself, I'm sorry that you are so immature and crazy!

After all that had just happened, he asked if I was going to make him a lunch to take to work with him, almost as if nothing had happened and everything was back to normal. I said, "You treat me like this and expect me to make you a lunch? No!" He got *really* mad. I was still on the couch holding my baby boy when he came over and punched me in the arm several times and choked me with his forearm. I got him away a little so his arm wasn't on my neck, but more on my chin, then I shoved him away with my hand on his face. I screamed at him 'what are you doing?!' He said he was going to kill me and that he didn't care anymore. I said with another shove, "You better *start* caring right now and think about what you're doing!" He backed off. He went outside and then came back in. He said he had cut the phone wires outside. He then remembered that there was a payphone down the street, so he demanded that I give him the pre-paid phone card that his dad had given us for Christmas. That wasn't the first time he'd kept our calling cards from me.

He started trying to be nicer after that. He told me he didn't want me to leave but since I wasn't acting nice or forgiving, he said he was taking the kids. He proceeded to put my baby boy in his car seat. He was crying because he was hungry and I was still nursing him. I told Dusty he was *not* taking the kids and that I needed to feed the baby. He hit my other arm to get me away from him. I assured him I wasn't leaving because I had nowhere to go anymore. He calmed down and said he felt hurt because he thought I respected Aaron and I never acted that way to him. I thought Dusty was extremely insecure and had to feel like he controlled everything by acting out of control. I had to wonder to myself about his sanity however, because even when he was calm and not angry, he had told me 'yes, I would kill you if you ruined my life financially by taking the kids and trying to get money out of me'.

His grandma paid his child support for him for his other daughter. She must not have realized that by trying to help him she was actually enabling his irresponsibility. All of her other grandkids felt like she favored him over everyone else. Maybe that was one reason he decided it was fine to act the way he did. He was rude to her too, but she would just take it and still do most everything he wanted. He told me he'd held her up in a chokehold against the wall once. I don't know how she still let him live with her. She told me I should just ignore his words and 'not receive them'. She said it was just Satan working through him. I guess *that's* how she did it. She told me she prayed all the time that I wouldn't 'fall apart and leave again'. I didn't exactly think *I* was 'falling apart'. Dusty was in her best interest, not me. It was really frustrating to me that she was always acting like I was the one that made all the difference in whether we made it or not. I guess Dusty told his family whatever he wanted to so they'd feel sorry for him and think I was the problem. He was pretty good at that. He could sure put up a great 'poor me' persona.

Dusty told me if I ever got pregnant again that I '*will* have an abortion'. I told him I couldn't do that because it would devastate me! He said it didn't matter and that he would slip me something to abort it or punch me in the stomach, but I would *not* have another baby because we couldn't afford it. He said if I didn't abort it, we would put it up for adoption. I couldn't do that either! He told everyone in his family that he had a vasectomy, which wasn't true. He said he didn't want me to get my tubes tied after I had our son because he figured it would be better if he was the one to have it done. I couldn't understand why he wouldn't just go get a vasectomy right then and prevent it all together. He did finally have it done about a year later, thankfully. I didn't think he should ever be allowed to have another child. He told me that as a teenager, he had slept with his stepsister all the time because they 'were both good looking and the same age and had suddenly been thrown together in the same house when his dad married her mom'. He said she had gotten pregnant and he'd helped her pay to get it aborted. He said he didn't know if it was his though because she had also been sleeping with her boyfriend.

Once, he sat and told our toddler daughter how I had almost aborted her. Of course she had no idea what he was talking about, but I could not believe he had the *audacity* to do such a thing! I wondered what life would be like for my kids in the future if he didn't change. A nightmare, that's what it would be!

He had me really confused. Whenever we were done fighting and he wasn't so angry anymore he would say he didn't mean anything he said. He would say he was just hurt and I shouldn't take everything he said so literally. How was it possible for him to be *so convincing* all the time?

I didn't know what to do. I only wanted to have a good marriage and not put my kids through the hell of having divorced parents. The hell I was in was getting worse though, and my kids could have possibly had one parent less if Dusty ever carried out his threats. I thought I must be stupid for staying and hoping. Hoping could have gotten me killed!

None of what had been happening seemed that bad until I wrote it down or talked about it. Everybody that heard about it could see clearly what I could not. It was far from a normal or healthy relationship. I just thought I should try to get us back into counseling, again. Dusty said he would do whatever it would take to make our relationship work. I made a list of reasons why I didn't leave and a list of why I should have.

Why I Don't Leave

He'll take the kids away.

I don't have any money.

I'll have to ask my family for help, again.

I don't have the energy to start over.

I can't make enough money to pay for daycare and my bills.

He's got my car.

I will feel sorry for him.

I love him.

I don't know where I can go.

He will miss the kids.

My heart will break.

I will be lonely.

I don't know how I will move my stuff.

I need help and money.

I don't know if I can do it on my own.

My family and friends are tired of helping me because I keep going back.

I just want to be happily married.

I want to do the things I've planned and dreamed of.

I don't want my kids to have divorced parents.

I don't want to have another relationship.

I have hope that things will change and get better.

Why I Should Leave

He calls me names, horrible names, and does so in front of the kids.

He yells and demands everything.

He tells me I'm slow, stupid, can't do anything right, that I'm lazy and that I don't deserve anything because I'm not making money.

He says I owe him everything because he has put a roof over my head, food in my mouth, and pays the bills.

He says I can't make it on my own and that I would have to live on welfare and be white trash without him.

He won't let me call or visit my friends or family; he says it costs him too much money for the gas and phone.

He puts all my family and friends down.

When I do talk to them, he stands right there and wants to know everything that is being said.

He holds me down all the time.

He scares me.

He won't give me money to get my prescription for anti-depressants sometimes and criticizes me for using them.

He threatens me all the time and tells me to leave.

He accuses me of sleeping with Aaron or having a boyfriend.

He says he will kill the guy and me if I ever did.

He says I should be shot.

He says he just needs a bullet in his head because his life is over since he met me and has kids. He says he can't do anything he wants to do now.

He blames me for everything that goes wrong in his life.

My kids will suffer more in this type of environment than by being out of it! They will witness domestic violence if I stay.

I don't want my kids growing up and thinking it's okay to yell and cuss and break things.

I'm starting to act like him by swearing and trying to be mean back.

If I have to depend on him, he can control me more.

I have too much to lose by just 'having faith and hoping' again.

I don't know how I am to know when he really has changed without risking so much.

I left not long after this, and went to live with my mom. Dusty immediately got into counseling in Nevada. He called me on a daily basis and talked to me for hours. I could rarely get a word in myself, and it was not easy to get him off the phone. I mostly just sat and listened. The thought of duct tape would come to mind; I might actually be able to stand him if he had a piece of it over his mouth. He wanted to tell me all about what he was learning.

After he'd been going to counseling on his own for a while, I joined him. He really laid on the pressure for me to come home. He said he believed in God, which he didn't before. He often said he could change with God's help. He read *'Hidden Keys to Loving Relationships'* and watched ten hours of video on that, he listened to four hours of *'Learning to Live Without Violence'* and ten hours of *'The Psychology of Winning'* on cassette tapes. He was very patient. I stayed with him off and on in May.

One day in the car, we were talking about people that did drugs and Dusty said he had used them when he was in high school. He said he would beat people up for some guy to get them to pay for their drugs. He said he had killed two people. I freaked! I told him I absolutely could not be with someone that had done something like that. I had a million thoughts racing through my mind. I was trying to think about what I was supposed to do with information like that. A half hour later he told me he was just testing me to see how I would react. He said he wanted to see if I would love him no matter what and that I had failed his test miserably. He just laughed about it like it was some funny joke. He said he hadn't really killed anyone and he just wanted to see what I would do. What a psycho. I told our counselor about this. She said she didn't believe he had actually killed anyone and that Dusty had what you would call 'black humor'. She then told Dusty that 'many people like Hanna do not accept that' and that he needed to watch what he said. I couldn't help but wonder about it in the back of my mind.

I moved back to Nevada soon after the counseling ended. I felt like Dusty had changed a lot and had really put forth a lot of effort into making things better. He was much more patient and tried hard to watch what he said. Aaron still didn't want the boys around Dusty. He said they could come and visit me at my mom's but they couldn't go to Nevada. I was supposed to have them for their summer visit. I took them to Nevada anyway for my weekend. He filed for a protective order for our boys and took me to court. I ended up getting part of my summer visit, but Aaron came and got them halfway through and said it was his turn for a weekend visit with them and that I couldn't deny him that. It was extremely stressful. He didn't let me have my other two weeks of visitation. Things were actually really good with Dusty and I that spring and summer though. At the time, I couldn't understand why Aaron wouldn't believe me.

Dusty figured it would be a good idea to have a yard sale toward the end of the summer and sell everything. He said we could use the money and that it would make it easier on him in case I left again. He just assumed that I'd probably leave again and then come back, which meant more things for him to pack and move.

August

One morning in August, Dusty woke up in a bad mood, which was not unusual. I was in the kitchen feeding my baby boy with a spoon. We were both sitting on the floor and my daughter was sitting a little way away from us. I had just gotten them out of the bathtub and they were both hungry. I didn't drain the water and get all the toys out of the tub when I was done because I was trying to hurry and dress them and get them in the kitchen to eat. Dusty didn't like it when I left the tub that way. He yelled at me to 'get my a-- in there and clean out the tub'. I was a little surprised at how he'd asked and it immediately offended me. I just ignored him. He kept yelling at me and I kept ignoring him. I wanted him to know I wasn't about to put up with that from him. He threw his boot across the room and it went right between me and my son. It could have hit either one of us. I could tell what was happening again and that it would only escalate if I didn't go clean out the tub. I went in there and threw the toys out on the floor and then got out of there. I didn't like being confined to a small room when he was angry. He yelled at me again to get back in there and clean up the water on the floor from the toys. I felt like Cinderella in there mopping while he stood over the top of me. I hated him for treating me like that again. I couldn't stand it any longer. I had given him too many chances and I knew I was going to leave as soon as I could. He knew he had messed up and was concerned about me leaving again. He was cautious, and watched me closely. I tried to act like his behavior didn't affect me that much and waited for him to go get in the shower. I turned up the stereo and threw some clothes in a pillowcase, so if he came out of the bathroom suddenly, he wouldn't be suspicious of me packing. Then all at once, I got my daughter in one arm and my son in the other, grabbed the pillowcase, and ran out to the car. I drove the three-hour drive to my mom's as fast as I could. I went about 90+ miles per hour on that long desolate desert road and kept checking my rearview mirror. I was so scared that I didn't even care if I got a ticket. I decided that would've actually been good because then I would've had a cop to help me! I was so afraid of what would happen if he followed and caught up to me. I didn't know if he would run me off the road to get me to stop or what he would do!   Nevertheless, I made it safely to my mom's.

Chapter 8

Away for Awhile

We lived with my mom and younger sister and I started a paralegal course that I could do at my own pace. It was a two-year program, but I intended to finish it quickly. I wanted to know more about laws and how to defend myself better in court if I had to. I knew I could use the degree and knowledge for myself and it would help me get a good job. I didn't date or go anywhere all winter. I talked to Dusty occasionally on the phone but he knew I didn't like him and didn't want to get back together. I was cold to him most of the time. I didn't want to be vulnerable or open and I built a big wall around myself. I still felt sorry for him in some ways and let him spend Christmas with us so he could be there with the kids. I felt torn as to whether I should get divorced yet or not. I couldn't quite cut my ties and I took marriage as a serious bond.

I received a letter from my friend while I was living with my mom:

Letter from Nicole:

Hey long lost pal, how the hell are you? I really do miss you and the good times we used to have. Everything is going a lot better for me now. I'm not seeing anybody. I'm not ready for another relationship right now. The only thing that got me through is that I kept telling myself that there was no reason to settle for someone who wanted to take out of a relationship more than he gave to it. I deserve more than that, I deserve the best, and so do you! I know that you are strong enough to get out of this for good. Please don't let me down! I love you too much to see you do what you have over the last 2 years. That is why I haven't been much for calling or visiting you. I hate it because I feel like I lost one of my best friends but it is better than seeing you live a lie. I know that sounds awful but it only sounds like what it is. I really miss your boys. In fact, I have a friend living there and I was going to ask Aaron if I could take them to McDonald's or something. They must be so big by now! I am really worried that you will go back to Aaron #2. Sorry, but that is who he reminds me of, only worse. Have you been thinking about going to counseling? I know you wanted to once. I know it would help you along the right road. Think about it. I don't mean to preach, and you know I'm the last one to try but I am so worried that if you ever do go back to Dusty he is going to kill you. I know you wanted to stick it out and you hoped that he would change. But in your heart, you knew he wouldn't. He's not the one! That is what I realized with my ex-boyfriend. I didn't want him being the father of my children. I saw how it affected him with his parents not being the example they should be and I turned around and ran! Now, I will get off my soapbox.

Heidi, I love you and I know you will make it. Please, please don't prove me wrong. Take care of yourself and your family. You have done the best thing for them all by leaving Dusty. He will only cause hard feelings and terrifying memories. You all deserve more. I am looking forward to seeing your kids, and most of all, you! Remember, what you believe, you will become. I will always be here for you.

I love you,

Nicole

Since the time my boys went to live with their dad and he wouldn't let them come back, I was always asking Aaron what I needed to do so I could have them back again. He would never really give me an answer. All I knew was that I needed to be stable and not be with Dusty. I did the best I could and hoped and prayed they would be with me again soon. Aaron let my younger son come and live with me the following January. He and his wife were in the process of moving to a different city and thought that would make the transition easier on him. I was overjoyed! I signed him up for karate and he did well in it. He was doing really well in school too. During the summer, I had to put the kids in daycare while I worked. It was rather difficult because Aaron told me not to use state assistance and Dusty didn't want me to use it either. Neither of them wanted the state coming after them for money. It came to a point however, when I felt like I really needed to. When I went in to talk to the state worker, I was under the impression that Aaron wouldn't know about the state helping me with daycare for our son. He never offered to help pay anything for him while he lived with me; we just agreed that neither of us would pay each other since we both had one child. I didn't think that was entirely fair because he made quite a bit more money than me, but I didn't argue about it. If it was just money that might keep my son from being able to live with me, I wouldn't say anything.

I finished my paralegal school in April and started working in a law office in May. We all moved into a bigger house nearby where there was more room for us and I was able to start paying my mom some rent. I loved my mom and it was nice to get to know her better and get closer to her. She helped me so much when I didn't know what else to do. I truly felt her love and acceptance of me. My job at the law firm was good, and overall, I was feeling pretty great about myself. I felt so happy to be free and to have my kids with me. My oldest son still lived with Aaron and I missed him dearly, but that was what he wanted. He was happy there and had lots of friends.

I finally filed for a divorce in June. With my training and working in a law office, I was able to do the paperwork myself. I dated a little bit in the summer and fall, but nothing came from it. I kind of hoped that by dating other people, it would help me get over Dusty easier and maybe keep him from bothering me or wanting me back. I needed some finalization. It was during this time that Dusty said he'd hired a detective to follow my every move. He named off a few places he said I'd recently been to, just to show me he was serious. He was hoping to catch me doing something wrong to use against me in court and to try to prove he could still exert control over me.

After dating a while, I would think I found someone that was just right, but was let down when they didn't feel the same way about me. I didn't want to think I was asking too much of someone because I had kids and ex-husbands. I felt rejected and like no one that I wanted would want me back. It was quite a lonely feeling. I had been trying to prove to myself that I could be with any one I wanted that met my standards and I didn't want to settle for anything less. I started wondering if Dusty was the best I could do.

In July, Aaron called saying he had gotten a bill from the state and wanted me to take care of it. I kind of brushed it off and forgot about it. I didn't think he should be making a big deal out of helping out with the daycare bill. He called again in August and was angry and rude, so I got defensive. After hanging up, I realized that it was stupid. I should just pay it so there wouldn't be any fighting. I tried to call him right back to tell him I would just pay the $600 for daycare but he wouldn't answer his phone. The next thing I knew, I got a call from my son's school saying that his dad had just come and picked him up. I was in complete shock. Aaron had taken my son from me out of anger! He'd told me to go ahead and register him in school for the year, and he had already been going for a week when this happened. He had been doing so well living with me! He was excelling in his karate class and was a happy boy. It was certainly not in his best interest to be yanked out of that. I was so angry and hurt and full of heartache. I did all I could legally to fight it, but by the time we had gone through the court just trying to change venue, my son had already been at his dad's for four months going to school. I felt like it wasn't in his best interest to take him back out of school again and I figured the courts would've looked at it the same way. Aaron told me years later that the reason he came and got my son wasn't because of the money, but because the state was going to change custody and give it to me since he had been living with me. He thought I was trying to be sneaky and had known that all along. I thought that was strange since he'd only complained about me taking care of the daycare bill and had come and got my son immediately after I said I wouldn't pay it. Aaron said he wouldn't lose control of his kids because he felt like he had lost control for a while when I was with Dusty. He said he would protect them and would *never* give up custody.

My divorce was final that October. I often went for walks in the canyon with my kids and my friend Shelly. We took my dog, Sam, with us too. He was a big yellow lab. I brought him home one day hoping my mom would be okay with having him there. She didn't seem to mind. He was a really good dog. I just loved him, and so did the kids! It was nice to be able to have a pet like him. Shelly and I talked a lot and it was really good for me to be able to do that. It helped me work through a lot of stuff. She often liked going to the local club/bar to dance. She didn't drink or swear or sleep around with people, she just liked to go have fun dancing. That wasn't really the best place for me to be, but it was fun going there. I didn't really ever drink. I still felt guilty however, because I had been told relentlessly by Dusty 'that's not what mom's are supposed to do', even though my kids were always at home and in bed, and my sister and my mom were there with them. The kids usually didn't even know I was gone.

Dusty started going to church and decided he wanted to get baptized that fall. I was completely astounded. After all the times he'd put me down for it and freely shared his negative opinion on the subject, I just couldn't believe it. He seemed quite humbled and was soon acting like a different person. He was kind, but not pushy, about getting back together. He said he was doing what he was doing regardless of what happened with us.

I met Andrew sometime during the winter. He had come into the law office needing some help and struck up a conversation with me. He asked me for my phone number. I really didn't want to give it to him but *I* didn't enjoy being rejected and I didn't want to make *him* feel that way, and he seemed like a decent guy. He was just my friend. He was really spiritual and kind and a good influence on me. I didn't want anything more from him than just a friendship though. I guess back then I just wasn't attracted to men that weren't swinging from the chandeliers.

I called Dusty in March to see if he was going to want to see the kids again soon. His last visitation before then had been at the end of January. He wasn't supposed to see the kids until he had taken the required Divorce Education Class. He said he had taken the class, but no certificate was ever sent to the court saying he did. I highly doubted he was telling the truth about that. He wanted to know how I would feel if he moved to Oklahoma for work. I told him to do whatever he wanted to do, but he wouldn't be able to see the kids as much if he moved that far away. He said he didn't see them much anyway, I would most likely get remarried again sometime, and that I probably already had someone lined up. He said even if I was divorced, I would be committing adultery if I got married again. He was always trying to quote bible verses to back up his statements. He kept asking questions about whether I had a boyfriend or not. I replied that I had a friend that was a guy, but that he was just a friend and I wasn't dating him. He freaked! He said he wanted to be released from all his parental rights and responsibilities immediately. I think he wanted me to state that I had a boyfriend just so he could say he wanted this release without feeling guilty about it. He went on to say if I didn't give him this, he would 'kill Andrew', he would 'beat his eyes shut and bury him', then he hung up on me. He called me again the next day to see if I had the papers drawn up yet. I told him, 'no' and he demanded to know why. I told him I didn't know if he was just mad and didn't mean it because he always said crazy things out of anger. He replied 'yes, he most certainly did mean it' and that I 'better give him what he wanted or he would kill Andrew'. I hung up on him. He was such a fool. He called again two days later to see if I had done the papers. I was not about to draw up these ridiculous papers he imagined he should have, and that a judge would be very unlikely to sign anyway. He made more threats to kill Andrew and accused me of sleeping with him. I told him I hadn't, and Andrew really *was* just a friend. It didn't matter to him what I said. Dusty said when he was through with Andrew I wouldn't even want to look at him again. He told me what a rotten mother I was and went on to ask me how I knew Andrew wouldn't abuse the kids. He demanded several times that I better give him what he wanted or Andrew was going to be killed and stated that he was ashamed I was the mother of his children. I told him 'vice versa' and that he could do the paperwork himself if he was that serious. He got mad and went on to say I should do it because I worked at a law firm and if I didn't help him write it, Andrew would pay. I told him I hoped he went to jail where he belonged, and hung up.

In the law firm where I worked, there were five attorneys. Two of them were only a couple of years older than me. I worked mostly for just one of them. Each attorney had his own paralegal to help them. The other attorney that was a couple of years older than me gave me tasks every once in a while too. He was flirtatious and winked at me a lot. At first, it was flattering to be getting attention from a nice looking attorney. I was suffering from low self-esteem and it was a bit gratifying. It was also quite unflattering because he was married and had a child and he held a respectable position in his church. He would ask me rather inappropriate questions and make a lot of suggestive comments and gestures when no one else could see him except me. I didn't have much respect for him. I would have been really angry if I was his wife. I asked him what he thought his wife would think of him asking me questions like that. He said he would never really do anything, but 'there was nothing wrong with having fantasies'. I went along with it a little. I felt intimidated. I didn't want him to *dislike* me, and I didn't want to lose my job - my job that gave me security. He told me once that if I ever told anyone, I would be working at Subway. I told him not to *ever* talk to me like that again and *not* to threaten me. He smiled and just kind of laughed it off. He was quite arrogant and acted like he ruled the whole firm. A girl called the office shortly after that looking for an attorney to represent her for a situation she was in that involved sexual harassment. I referred her to him, hoping he would see the light. He would have to be forced to look at what could happen to a person that was behaving that way and defend her for something he was doing himself. It was the least I could do.

I told Dusty about it once when we were talking on the phone, which proved to be a really bad idea. He told me I had better not go to work the next day or he would come in and tell everyone there everything I had said. I believed he would because he had gone into Andrew's work once looking for him and they called the cops because of the way Dusty was acting. I didn't tell my work the real reason for my leaving. Nonetheless, Dusty took care of that for me later on down the road. He called the main attorney and told him everything. I found out afterward that the flirtatious attorney was questioned about it and he told them that I was 'living in a fantasy world' and had 'made it up'.

He went on to continue this behavior with other girls that went to work there.

Dusty wanted me to come back to him. In a way, he felt like a hero by getting me out of the law firm I was working at. I thought his intentions were good to a point, but really he was helping take away my independence. He sent me flowers and wanted to talk all the time. I felt pressured by Andrew too because he kept wanting to be more than just friends. I didn't want to be with him like that. I enjoyed his friendship, but he said he couldn't really date other people and be my friend. I told him he *should* date other people and not worry about me. I didn't want to hold him back.

I didn't have a job and I didn't know what to do anymore. It didn't seem to matter if I was stable or not to Aaron, he wasn't letting my boys come back. I thought maybe if I went to Salt Lake there would be more job opportunities at one of the law firms there. I figured since Dusty had gotten baptized, was going to church and trying to become a better person, that he would be different. He also said he had started taking some medication to help him with his anger problem. I thought he would be safe to be around.

I went back to Salt Lake in May. I told Dusty I absolutely would *not* live with him though. I wasn't having much luck with finding an apartment that I could afford, so I planned to live in the 36' RV on his grandma's property until I could get enough money together and find a place. I paid her three month's rent in advance because I didn't want her telling me what to do and I didn't want to 'owe' her anything. I wasn't happy about it, but I had to put my stuff in storage at her other house. Dusty was not supposed to live there with me nor stay the night with me. I told him that was too much for me and I needed my own space. He agreed to respect my wishes. I took my dog with me and he stayed in the kennel with the other dog there. It seemed like it was all going to work out okay.

I decided it would be nice to start going to church again. I'd been inactive for many years and I thought Dusty would be happy to go too, since he'd gotten baptized and all. When

Sundays came, he always had something else to do and pretty much had no interest in going to church altogether. I felt kind of disappointed. He later told his mom that he'd only gotten baptized to try and get me back.

My cell phone was one of the first things to go, but not before he'd called everyone on my contact list to find out who they were and how they knew me. He said he 'accidentally' dropped it in the sink of water, which ruined it completely. It must have been coincidental that he happened to be mad at me at the time. I also found out that the 'medication he was taking for his anger problem' was only ibuprofen.

One night, Dusty was upset because I wouldn't let him stay in my RV to watch television and because I wanted to be left alone. He said he wanted to 'talk'. I wouldn't let him in regardless. He kept banging on the door and shaking the RV. He left for a short while and came back saying my dog was out of the kennel and I had better get out there and put him up or he was going to shoot him. I was too scared to come out. I knew he was just saying that to get me to open the door. He was making a scene. The nearest neighbor was a quarter mile away, but I was sure they could hear him yelling. A few minutes later, his gun went off and he said he had shot my dog! My heart dropped, but I stayed in my RV. I was too afraid to come out to check on my dog, even if he had been shot. I waited for a while. It was about midnight when I heard some talking outside and saw flashlights shining around in the dark. I finally came out to see what was going on and found that there were cops out walking around with Dusty. Apparently the neighbors had called them because of the noise disturbance. Dusty was telling the officers that he had been yelling at the dog and shot at a skunk, and of course, they believed him. I was relieved to find that my dog was perfectly fine and running around happily. Dusty's grandma came outside and didn't say much of anything until the cops left. She knew that Dusty hadn't told them the truth. He told her I didn't put my dog up, and who knows what else. All she had to say to me about it was, 'you need to make sure you put your dog up', which she said as if she was really annoyed with me. I couldn't believe it! I figured she was mad because she thought I was the one to call the cops. I told her I hadn't. How could I? I didn't have a phone. She either didn't believe me or didn't care. I hated her for not caring and for enabling Dusty all the time. At first, when I had gotten there, she was nice and everything was good. Then little by little, we both just started to annoy each other. All she seemed to care about was Dusty and his selfish, bratty requests.

It didn't seem to matter at all to Dusty that I didn't want to be around him much and wanted my own space. As far as he was concerned, he had me back. On Memorial Day, he had been insulting me and calling me names and I was trying to ignore him. He backed me up against the door in his grandma's kitchen. He yelled right in my face and acted like he was going to hit me. He punched the door right next to my head instead, which left a hole in it. I went outside because I didn't want to talk to him and just wanted to get away from him, so he figured that meant I was planning on leaving. He told me I would *die* before I left *him*. With that, he put me in a headlock, and while holding me under his arm, he ran toward the house like he was going to bash my head into the brick siding. He stopped right before I hit the wall. I turned around and smacked him and screamed at him to *NEVER* threaten me with my life like that again! He choked me and hit me behind my left ear. He held me down in the dirt and spit on me. I spit back at him and tried to throw dirt in his face. He stood up and started kicking and throwing dirt back. Anytime he came near me, I kicked. I got his knee once and it buckled. He finally left me alone and stopped acting so violent. He changed his approach to me and tried to calm me down because he had never seen me so upset. I was hysterical. It was then that he suggested we kill each other with the guns in the house. I can't remember anything after that.

June

Dusty had been insulting me and my family again, so I didn't want to talk to him. He kept following me around talking and spitting out insult after insult. I told him I had nothing to say to him and to leave me alone. He followed me into my trailer anyway. He wasn't getting the response he wanted from me, so he pushed me into the wall and hit me twice. He tried to choke me and then grabbed a handful of my hair on the top of my head and dragged me to the trailer door telling me he was 'kicking me out' and that he would have a chat with his grandma to make sure I left. Our two children watched the whole thing happen. Of course, he was ever so sorry, but he said I could not leave him just because of what had happened. He got a knife out of the drawer and said I would have to kill him before I could leave and if I didn't, he wouldn't let me go with the kids.

I left him the following Monday night while he was in his house taking a shower. It was pretty scary. I drove really fast and went to Nicole's. I stayed there for a couple of days. I went and filed for a protective order and went to the state for some help with money so I could start over, *again*. I explained my situation to the lady and she told me if I didn't leave Dusty 'now' that my kids would be taken away. I had every intention of leaving. I went back to where my mom lived. I didn't have any of my stuff but I didn't care; I was just glad to be out of there.

Andrew helped me go back to get my stuff out of the storage house that Dusty's grandma had. After that, I took my mom's truck and a cop to his grandma's place to get my things out of the RV. While we were there, she tried to act nice, I believe only because there was a cop with me. I had to hurry really fast because the cop didn't want to wait long. I just needed to get what I had left in the RV. I went over to go inside and found that it had been locked. She said the key she had to the RV didn't work, which I didn't believe. I told her to stop messing around and open the door. She fiddled with the keys for a while and finally the door opened. She tried to help me pack but was throwing stuff in the back of the truck, which I asked her not to do because I had to reorganize it so it would all fit. I knew that whatever I left there, she would give away to donations. I was glad we'd already loaded the trailer. We had gone to get my other stuff without telling her because I was afraid if I had told her beforehand, she would have made it difficult.

I got into a nice apartment when I moved back. It was government subsidized, so I was able to afford it. I couldn't get a job at another law firm in that town because usually you would have to wait at least eighteen months to work within a hundred miles of a firm you'd previously been employed with; some cases might conflict with each other. I worked as a waitress and at a tanning salon for several months while keeping an eye out for something better. It was quite depressing to me how my life was turning out up to that point in time. I wondered if I would ever be happy.

My life seemed to be going nowhere. I was working in restaurants and I hated that the atmosphere was so unprofessional sometimes. Waitressing was not my greatest talent. I had dated a little bit but found no one I was really interested in. I don't know if it was because I was young and impatient, but I felt like things always needed to be happening for me 'right now'. I was feeling pretty down in the dumps that winter and it was especially hard around Christmas time. I called Dusty up one day and asked him if we could get back together. I'd had time to regain my strength and confidence and was certain that we could do it right this time. How quickly I had forgotten all the bad things that happened throughout our relationship!

Chapter 9

Last Chance

It felt great getting back together again after being on my own for so long and having it be so difficult. It was just a few days before Christmas when I moved to Salt Lake. We stayed at Dusty's mom's house for the first two months until we could get a place of our own. He was working as a horse trainer and I helped him out by cleaning some of the stalls. I also worked a temporary job helping out with the Olympics' committee.

We moved to the southern part of Salt Lake in a place where there was an apartment attached to a barn. It was a really nice barn with a lot of beautiful horses. Dusty trained them, taught riding lessons, and helped the owner out with whatever else needed to be done.

Dusty's grandma had been letting us use a little car that had been donated to the ranch ministry and Dusty wanted me to sell my car. I didn't drive my car much, but I really wanted to keep it...just in case. His grandma thought it was pretty ridiculous for me to want to keep it but I felt like I would have no control if I gave it up. I think they both knew that, which may have been one of the reasons they wanted me to sell it. Dusty also tried to tell me that it was *his* car now because he was the one that had put money into having it fixed. The title was in my name though, and I wasn't going to change it.

He went through my clothes and threw away the ones he didn't like. He took me to buy some new ones because he said I needed to look like a 'horse trainer's wife'. Of course if I ever left him, he would be keeping anything he had bought for me because 'they were *his* since *he* paid for them, and if I didn't want to be with him then I didn't deserve to have them'.

Dusty started complaining a lot about money and it seemed I would never hear the end of how he worked and I needed to earn more. I didn't know what more I could do. I had two babies to take care of. I was cooking and cleaning and trying to help him outside with the horses whenever I could, which wasn't easy with two toddlers. I really hated working along side him because he was so impatient with me. He'd tell me things like he was 'going to break my thumbs for holding the reins wrong' and never had anything good to say. I really wanted to find something I could do from home, but I didn't know what.

A couple of his clients were young women that he referred to as 'buckle bunnies' and he would joke about how they were all after him. He thought he was quite good looking and was fairly conceited about it. He was always looking at himself in his truck mirror and fixing his mustache. It was impossible to give him compliments because 'he already knew it'. I found his arrogance to be quite a turn off.

He wouldn't let me sleep in when he had to get up at 6 a.m. He would turn the stereo up really loud in the other room, flip all the lights on, and pull my blankets off. He would go outside and do some work, then come back in to make sure I was up. He wouldn't let me sit on the couch to read or watch television while he was at work either. I just wanted to watch the news in the morning to help me wake up. I never was a very good morning person. He would yell at me and threaten to break the television if it was ever on; we could only watch it when *he* wanted to. I didn't watch it much anyway, but I wanted him to stop trying to control everything I did and quit treating me like I couldn't govern myself. Once, he asked if I needed to take speed or something to get me going and seemed to be seriously suggesting it. I didn't think an illegal drug was the answer. I thought he was an idiot. He contradicted himself so much. Normally he was always so against drug users and constantly criticized a couple of my siblings that had had a problem with using them in the past. He didn't care if they weren't using anymore, 'our kids would never be around them', which was actually just a good excuse for him to keep me away from my family.

It seemed that anytime I wanted to call or see my family, we couldn't afford it, according to Dusty. In his opinion, that should've been my last priority. He didn't like anyone in my family and continually criticized them. I knew he felt insecure because none of them liked him, so he just acted as if he didn't care what they thought of him. He would point out any issues or faults they had and try to convince me that I should just cut them out of my life. That seemed pretty easy for him to do with some of his own family.

As time went on, it seemed he was growing more and more discontent. I don't know if I just brought out the worst in him or if it was just his own issues that he didn't know how to deal with. Nothing I did seemed to ever be good enough. He was short on patience and acted like he controlled everything. I felt like a lion in a cage. He would want to keep me up really late to talk when I didn't want to. He wouldn't allow me go to sleep. He would sit and bother me by poking me, he'd talk right in my face, pull the blankets off me, turn on the light, yell, push me off the bed, pour water on me, and say things to try and get me angry.

He started disliking his job for reasons I am not really sure of. He said he wasn't being treated fairly or getting what he wanted as far as 'trainer recognition' and he wanted to leave. It seemed he went through jobs often and always had some reason that it was their fault he wanted to quit (or got fired?). We had nowhere else to go but to his Grandma's, but I absolutely refused to go back there again, which consequently caused a lot of problems.

I remember him being afraid I'd leave and he held me down and spit in my face. He hit me behind my ear ('because', he said, 'it wouldn't leave a mark that you could see this time') and locked me in the back bedroom. For the second time, he told me I should do him and the kids a favor and commit suicide. I was truly at my bitter end. I had lost almost everything. I was done trying with him. He wasn't changing and I was emotionally drained.

The last night we were together, he said he didn't care if I left, but I wasn't taking the kids, and I couldn't have anything his grandma had given us, including the vacuum that I had gotten for Mother's Day. I was used to not getting to keep any gifts he'd given me, so I didn't really care about that. I couldn't have my desk or the washer and dryer either. He said that 'we were through' and he took the washer and dryer to his grandma and told her to give them to donations. He was mad at me because he thought I was being ungrateful since I didn't want to live at his grandma's house. I knew I just could *not* do that again. We had been moving all of our stuff into a storage unit all day and almost had everything out of the apartment. He wanted to spend the night at his grandma's instead of our house so he would have a bed to sleep in, so he drove us to her house later that evening.

I didn't want to spend the night at his Grandmas, especially after what we had gone through during the day, and I wouldn't be able to leave like I wanted to if we stayed there. I was holding my little boy and sitting in the cab of the truck because I didn't want to get out. Dusty was standing outside the door holding our daughter when he threw some apple juice, along with the bottle, in my face. While trying to get the keys to the truck from me, he twisted my wrist so hard I thought it would break. He always said if I ever took his truck and left, he would report it stolen and have me put in jail.

I finally talked him into going back to our house and we slept on the floor. He held onto my belt loop to keep hold of me during the night. I guess he figured it would wake him if I moved his hand. He was a deep sleeper though, so I waited until he fell asleep to make my escape. I had a large black garbage bag full of our most-needed things ready and waiting next to the back door. Since we were already in the process of moving, the garbage bag was not conspicuous. I knew that what I'd packed might be the only things I ever left with. I didn't care. I just wanted to get away safely and have my kids with me.

I couldn't believe I had gotten myself to this dreadful place. Hadn't I learned anything? Someone once said that at first you are a victim, after that you are a volunteer. It must have been easy for them to say that, not having gone through the same situation. I always thought I was doing the right thing when I went back. I had a million reasons for staying and going back and they all seemed legitimate to me at the time.

I was so scared that he would catch me trying to leave. What then? What would he do to me? I surely didn't want to find out! I knew the risk of getting caught. I could have been killed. It seemed that was the point of rage he could easily get to if I was ever to leave him, and he had let me know it many times. In the times I had left before, I had gotten away safely enough. I feared the worst if he awoke during my getaway this time, even though in the past he had always been deeply sorry for how he had acted. He'd always managed to convince me to come back with pleading, tears, flowers, and promises. I would then feel as if I had gained some power over the situation. I thought I could handle it better the next time. I got stronger and more confident when I was away from him. Unfortunately, each time I went back, it was only to be torn down worse than the time before. My life depended on *this* escape.

I felt such an immense amount of guilt for what my kids had gone through, what *I* had put them through by staying in the situation, because of my naivety, low self-esteem, and insecurities. If only I had paid attention to the warning signs in the beginning!

I ever so carefully and quietly picked up the kids one at a time and snuck them out to my car. Once I had both of them buckled in, I felt a tremendous amount of relief come over me! I quickly locked the doors and rolled the car down the driveway without starting it. When I got out to the road, I started my car and sped away as fast as I could and went to my parent's house three hours away. It was finally the end of that six year relationship.

It's okay to fall apart for a little while. You don't always have to pretend to be strong, and there is no need to constantly prove that everything is going well. You shouldn't be concerned with what other people are thinking either – cry if you need to – it's healthy to shed your tears. The sooner you do, the sooner you will be able to smile again. Unknown.

Chapter 10

Starting Over

I lived with my parents for two months and then moved into a duplex near my two brothers in the same town. It helped me feel safer knowing they were so close. I had to use some state assistance to get started, but I didn't care. I felt like it was there for people like me. I wasn't going to take advantage of it; I just needed the boost to help get me on my feet again.

I filed a protective order against Dusty and the last time I saw him was in the courthouse three months after I had left. He was pretty upset with me for getting the order against him. He made a comment to me upon leaving the courtroom, right after he'd been ordered to stay away from me and not talk to me. He then drove past my brother's houses a few times (he didn't know I had my own duplex near them) just to prove to me that 'no piece of paper could stop him'. I called the police and told them what was happening and they came and patrolled the neighborhood. Thankfully, Dusty did not return.

I still didn't have any of my things that were left behind in the storage unit in Salt Lake and Dusty refused to let me get them. We had only a few clothes and personal things and some of the kid's toys in my new duplex. I was still glad to be gone from him even if I didn't have anything. Some of my neighbors from the church donated furniture to me and that really helped a lot! I was so grateful for the support I had around me.

Dusty had often threatened to beat up my dad and brothers because they were the ones likely to help me move my stuff. My dad offered to go get my things anyway, regardless of anything Dusty had threatened. He was not intimidated by him. My dad, my stepmom, and my sister-in-law drove a truck to Salt Lake and went to the storage unit to get my things. Dusty was supposed to tell the manager to let them get my stuff. They called Dusty when my parents arrived and he immediately drove to the storage unit, which wasn't part of the arrangement. As soon as my dad saw him he ran over and punched him right in the face and knocked his sunglasses off! Dusty went running down the street yelling, "Help! Someone call 911!"

Right or wrong, I couldn't help but get a little joy from that. He pressed charges against my dad. My dad didn't mind having to pay a fine for what he did, but he was lucky he didn't have to go to jail. Dusty later said that he didn't want to fight my dad because he knew he had heart problems. Yeah, right. Needless to say, I still didn't get to have any of my things out of the storage.

Aaron offered to help me go get my stuff a couple of weeks later. He had a horse trailer and truck and said he would drive it over to Salt Lake and help me load it. When we got there it was pretty late and I had to knock on the manager's door to have them let us through the gate. I didn't want to go during the day and take the chance of Dusty showing up. Once I told them who I was they were rather short with me and said I could only be in there for thirty minutes and then they were going to close the gate, and that was after I *begged* them to let me get my stuff! I wondered what else Dusty had told them because they were not nice about it at all and almost made me leave with nothing.

I found that he had put a new, much larger lock on the storage door thinking I wouldn't be able to open it. I had come prepared for that though, and brought a large pair of metal cutters. I had to hurry and get as much loaded as I could. It was really frustrating because I couldn't take enough time to load it right to make the best fit. I didn't get to take everything, but almost, and that was okay. It was just stuff. It could always be replaced.

Dusty took his visitation the first weekend after court. It had to be arranged through a third party. My daughter was having some medical issues and I passed on the directions the doctor had given me and stressed the importance of them being followed. I was worried about sending the kids, but I had no choice. He didn't follow any of the medical advice that he was given for her. The next time he wanted visitation, he gave me a really short notice and hadn't been consistent previously. I was unable to meet when he wanted to, so he gave up altogether. After that, he was constantly wanting me to have someone, anyone, adopt them. He didn't care who it was, even if it was my dad. He just wanted to be released from any responsibility required of him. He'd threatened me so much with killing me if I 'ruined his life financially and got state assistance', that I didn't ask him for a dime. The state didn't go after him either because of the special circumstances. It wasn't fair, but it kept me safe. There are some things I just had to let go of and let God take care of.

My kids had a hard time sleeping at night for about a year and a half after moving and my daughter was often quite distraught anytime I left to go somewhere without her, even if it was just to the gas station for a few minutes. My littlest boy, bless his heart, called me a b---- a couple of times when he was mad. He was only three years old and was merely repeating what he had heard. I had to talk to him about using nice words and that name-calling was not okay. He is a really sweet, tenderhearted young man now. My two older boys still lived with their dad but I saw them a lot more often and without any worry of Dusty being around! Aaron frequently brought up Dusty and how he didn't think he could trust me to have the boys live with me again. I understood and didn't blame him for feeling that way. It did come to a point in time however, when I had to tell him he could no longer use that against me. I had been stable and doing quite well and Dusty had been out of my life for quite some time. I felt like it was beginning to be an excuse. He didn't bring him up anymore after I asked him to stop doing that. I traveled to the boy's hometown each chance I had and watch them play football or their wrestling matches. They were with me at my house every other weekend. It was so wonderful to be able to do what I wanted without having to ask permission or be told 'no' for one reason or another.

I suffered from post traumatic stress syndrome for several years but have finally been able to work through that. I would shake uncontrollably whenever I started talking about anything that had happened and was fairly sensitive to anything reminding me of it, including movies, music, the way people talked, men that resembled or acted like Dusty, and smells, to name a few. I loved horses before being with Dusty but hated the smell and anything that had to do with them for a long time afterwards. I don't feel that way now; I am looking forward to owning them again and enjoying the freedom and joy that comes with riding and taking care of them.

I started counseling and got a job as a paralegal. My kids started school and life was pretty good. I made the decision that I was going to 'choose' to be happy! I learned some incredibly interesting things in counseling. I had not been aware of how some of the things I had been through were actually considered abusive. I learned all about the cycle of abuse, what constituted as abuse, and what characteristics and beliefs the batterer and victim typically held. Before going to counseling, I remember being in the courtroom for the protective order hearing and the judge had asked me how many incidents there had been throughout the course of our relationship. I hadn't kept track; there were too many! I didn't know if 'being held down' counted as abuse and asked the judge. The people in the courtroom just sort of smiled in disbelief. Yes, I was told, it certainly did count. In that case, I guessed there had been maybe fifty incidents of just that type of abuse alone. The judge said the number of incidents wasn't really all that important. He said only one incident could have happened and caused me to fear for my life or safety and would have been enough for a protective order. I really could not believe how many different types of abuse I had put up with and had minimized the severity of.

I eventually returned to school to get trained in medical transcription, as that was a job I could do from home, and got hired before I finished school.

I met the most wonderful man, and we have now been happily married for seven years! Our relationship is healthy. We are *equal* partners with trust, respect, honesty, shared responsibilities, responsible parenting and positive role modeling, our money decisions are made together, we make compromises when needed, and there is *never* threatening behavior. I *always* feel safe and protected! I love that I can just be me and it's always okay!

We've been through some especially difficult hardships over our years together and I know that I couldn't have gotten through them without someone as kind, caring, and loving as him. You never know what life will bring your way and I am ever so grateful to have a husband like mine. His patience and understanding and ability to always allow me to experience life in my own way has truly been a miracle to me. I wish I had known what kind of life was possible for me back when I felt I didn't deserve any better. It's true, we don't know what we've been missing until it arrives!

Difficulties

After Aaron had married his 3rd wife, he had to go to Iraq and wanted to leave my boys there with her and not with me. I really didn't think that was the right thing to do since he'd just barely married her and hadn't been with her long. I strongly felt my boys should be with me while their dad was away. They divorced three months into their marriage and he *still* didn't want the boys to live with me. He would've had them stay with friends instead of me if he could have. I know he was afraid that if they lived with me, they might not want to move back when he returned from Iraq. I didn't believe for a second that he was afraid of them being in some kind of jeopardy with me and my husband. I felt it was all about money and control. I had to take him to court in order to get my boys while he was away for six months. The whole thing was exceedingly stressful on me and quite hard on the boys.

Aaron was *extremely* upset with me while he was gone, mostly over the amount of child support he had to pay, which he made quite clear. I told him after court to just pay half of what he was supposed to so he wouldn't be so troubled. He angrily said he would pay half, but not because I was being nice and telling him he didn't have to, but because I 'owed' it to him. I told him to go ahead and just pay what he'd been court ordered then and he could figure out what he thought I 'owed' him and let the judge decide on the matter. I'd never seen him so bitter and angry. He believed I 'owed' him because 'he had to be responsible and earn money to provide for the boys while they lived with him and I should have had to do the exact same'. I was doing everything I could. I paid my child support to him and helped out with extras whenever I was able to. I told him *he* was the lucky one to have had the privilege of having the boys live with him! Why couldn't he see that?

While he was away and my boys were living with me, my oldest son got into some trouble. I did not have Aaron's support with anything, as he couldn't get past his resentment towards me. He blamed me for everything that seemed to go wrong. However, my son hadn't been doing well at either of our houses. I am grateful to this day that he did get into trouble because he was placed on house arrest and it was the best time of my life with him! We were exceptionally close and had many long talks, sometimes late into the early morning hours. I was always so proud of him. He was an 'A' student, excelled in sports, had lots of friends, and was well-liked by all those he came in contact with. He was a remarkably good-looking and intelligent young man. He was quite humorous and loved laughing and sharing his spirited personality.

I have never been so utterly shocked and devastated than the night a police officer came to my house to tell me my dearly loved son had committed suicide. He was barely sixteen years old at the time. It's been more than five years now since that happened, but I still think about him every single day and miss him more than words can describe. My faith has been significantly tested over the last few years and I've been forced into opening my mind to find what my truth is.

I'm not sure what Aaron was going through at the time, but I'm sure our son's death took a huge toll on him. I feel like he must have been angry, and lashing out at me was all he knew to do. We spent the next year and three months fighting each other in court. I felt like the time, money, and heartache I spent on continually having to defend myself in court over something so unnecessary was a large form of injustice. I was forced to hire an attorney and had to keep having paperwork drawn up each time Aaron sent something new. Needless to say, it was all especially difficult to go through after just losing my older son. Of course, all Aaron had tried to dispute ended up exactly the way I told him it would in the beginning. He seemed quite pleased though in trying to make my life as miserable as he was.

Over the next few years my husband and I were greatly affected by the recession that swept over the country, especially with the line of work he had been in for so many years. He was a drywall contractor and also worked in the oil fields doing gas flow-back testing, both of which came to a screeching halt.

During that same time, we both got Lyme disease (from tick bites) and it had gone unnoticed until after it was too late to take antibiotics to have it cured. My husband had symptoms show up first and was discouraged when the doctors were unable to find a diagnosis. Lyme disease mimics a lot of other diseases and symptoms and is hard to test for after a period of time has passed. It leaves you with joint pain, nerve pain, overwhelming fatigue, and several other issues. When my symptoms showed up shortly after his, I had a blood test done and it was positive for Lyme. We'd both had bites that formed a bulls-eye rash, typical of a tick bite. My husband could recall when he'd been bitten, but I was vague on when mine had occurred. We spent a lot of time camping in the mountains and had come across ticks several times. My husband had also come across them quite often while working out in the oilfield. Nevertheless, we hadn't known a thing about Lyme disease and dismissed the bites quickly. It was easy to just assume we had the flu as an after-affect that soon follows getting bitten. The most discouraging part of all, was having doctor after doctor tell us they didn't know what was wrong and that 'there is no Lyme disease in Utah'. We've done a tremendous amount of research and are still trying to find a treatment that works. Homeopathic remedies have seemed to be the most helpful thus far.

As a result of the Lyme disease, my husband got quite depressed with not being able to do what he had been capable of previously. His legs would cause him so much pain at times, and he was so tired all the time, that eventually it was difficult to even get him out of bed. He didn't have hardly any work available to do, so he didn't have the motivation he needed to get up and get going. It was really hard to watch him go through that and not know how to help him. Eventually, he sought out another job, was hired, and is now a supervisor there, which has been a blessing.

My husband's father was diagnosed with cancer and recently passed away. He was his best friend. We're glad he's not suffering anymore, but as it is with death, we are left with heartache and grief because we will miss him dearly.

We've grown so much closer to each other going through all these things together, which is amazing to me. I could not imagine going through it all with someone I was in an unhealthy relationship with!

My husband adopted my two youngest children and treats them like his own. He had two children of his own when he met me and I was able to adopt his younger one at the same time he adopted mine. What a wonderful day that was! What we've been through in our previous relationships has helped us to fully appreciate each other and what we have now.

Today our children all seem to be amazingly well-adjusted and happy! We've lived in the same house and neighborhood since we married, which I believe has provided our kids with the stability and security they desperately needed in their lives. My older son lives with me again and is a remarkable young man. We have our daily routines and activities and the kids are free to play and explore and enjoy life! There is a peace and comfort in our home that always makes it feel like a refuge from the rest of the world. I *love* that!

I am quite close to my other family members. It's nice living in the same town with so many of them. We get together for barbeques almost every weekend during the summers. We also get together for birthday celebrations, camping trips, and for each holiday. We are all still the best of friends! It's reassuring to always have someone close to talk to and to know they will always be there for you in any situation.

I've been keeping in touch with Ray over the last few years and our relationship has been developing into a wonderful friendship. We have a lot of laughs together over text messaging!

I have survived the trials in my life with the help of God, my family and friends, and outside resources. I've learned so many great lessons from those trials and I'm grateful to still be here to share them. I strongly believe we are here to learn and grow and I understand that it isn't what happens in our lives that matters nearly as much as how we handle those things and what we learn from them. I try not to be hateful or angry, that would only cause me to waste precious energy on something useless. I know that Aaron and Dusty each have their own issues to work through or overcome and I don't need to be a part of that, but I can forgive them and realize we are all here on our own journey. I have no room to judge, only room to keep myself safe. I would rather be out living my life to its fullest and being happy, than spending time worrying about things I cannot change. I am actually incredibly *thankful* for my life experiences because they've made me the strong person I am today! It's now been more than nine years since I left that destructive cycle and started my new life. It's so amazing to know *there really are happy endings!*

Chapter 11

How You Can Help Yourself or Someone Else

The things that made the difference for me in being able to stay away from Dusty included getting started in school, working a new job I enjoyed, setting goals, doing my favorite hobbies (I love writing poetry and lyrics, singing, and cooking), having the kids start activities, having family nearby to talk with each day and having their love and support, knowing how much my *kids* had already been affected by being in that relationship, getting educated and counseled about the cycle of abuse, and the stability and confidence I was quickly gaining. If it hadn't been for those things, I would have probably gone back to him again out of hopelessness or despair.

If you want to help someone in this type of situation, the best advice I could give you is to *educate* yourself and help *them* get educated on the matter too. Listen to them! If they tell you about what is happening, it may be hard for them to open up for fear they won't be believed or because they are embarrassed! The first step for the victim is *acknowledging the danger* of the situation they are in, and if they are willing to talk about it, that is a huge step in the right direction. There are lots of websites that can be utilized for this topic. Print off some copies for them, but take care not to leave those copies where the abuser would find them; that alone could cause problems for the victim. I've included a few helpful websites at the end of this book. Give them this book! It has a wealth of useful information! Help them regain confidence in themselves. Remind them of their talents and good traits. Help them get involved again in the things they enjoy doing. Do not judge them if they go back. Love them and let them know you are there any time they need you. Provide them with emergency phone numbers, including the National Abuse Hotline (included on page 140). Help them create a *safety plan* (guidelines on page 135). Offer your moral support if they need to go to counseling, to the police, to a lawyer, or to court. If you are a spiritual person, PRAY for them! It's never as simple as just getting angry and telling them not to go back or withholding your love and support, and it's never something you should take personally, even if it does feel that way to you when they go back to the abuser. The power involved in them going back to their abuser is far stronger than them trying to please their family and friends...or themselves. You cannot 'rescue' them even if it does hurt to watch them go through this. Ultimately it is up to the victim to decide to do something about their situation.

My advice to you if *you* are the one in this situation is to educate yourself! There *is* help out there. You can file for a protective order and it won't cost you anything. Go to the nearest police station and fill out a report. Have pictures taken of your bruises or injuries. Go to the emergency room to be checked so your case will be on file there. Keep a journal hidden so you can keep track of dates and incidences. Writing down what you are going through might help you see what is happening more clearly. All these things will help you in court! Call and talk with a victim advocate. The police station can give you a number to reach one. They will help you fill out any and all necessary paperwork, they will go to court with you, and they will have excellent advice for you, including other ways to get the help you need! Find out where the nearest women's shelter is. They are often nice facilities and kept secret so perpetrators are not likely to find them. They are locked and secured for your protection and it is unlikely for the perpetrator to get in. You can take your kids with you. They provide food and clothing and any other necessities you may need. There are people there to help counsel you in what you can do to help yourself and your children. Call them and ask them any questions you have! Your victim advocate will have a number to reach them. State assistance is available for you. It can help you get into your own residence and get back on your feet. There are programs to help you get further education so you are able to get a better job if needed. Contact your church. They often have programs, counseling services, and donation items to help you when starting over!

If you choose to stay, create a safety plan! There are guidelines for that on page 135. You are not alone. It is *not* your fault if someone chooses to abuse you! Know that *you and your children,* if you have them, *are worth it* to be *happy* and to *always* feel safe!

~The End~

"One of the greatest discoveries a person makes, one of their great surprises, is to find they can do what they were afraid they couldn't do." - Henry Ford

Safety Plan Guidelines

These safety suggestions have been compiled from safety plans distributed by state domestic violence coalitions from around the country. Following these suggestions is not a guarantee of safety, but could help to improve your safety situation.

Personal Safety with an Abuser

- Identify your partner's use and level of force so that you can assess danger to you and your children before it occurs.

- Try to avoid an abusive situation by leaving.

- Identify safe areas of the house where there are no weapons and there are ways to escape. If arguments occur, try to move to those areas.

- Don't run to where the children are, as your partner may hurt them as well.

- If violence is unavoidable, make yourself a small target; dive into a corner and curl up into a ball with your face protected and arms around each side of your head, fingers entwined.

- If possible, have a phone accessible at all times and know what numbers to call for help. Know where the nearest pay phone is located. Know the phone number to your local battered women's shelter. Don't be afraid to call the police.

- Let trusted friends and neighbors know of your situation and develop a plan and visual signal for when you need help.

- Teach your children how to get help. Instruct them not to get involved in the violence between you and your partner. Plan a code word to signal to them that they should get help or leave the house.

- Tell your children that violence is never right, even when someone they love is being violent. Tell them that neither you, nor they, are at fault or are the cause of the violence, and that when anyone is being violent, it is important to stay safe.

- Practice how to get out safely. Practice with your children.

- Plan for what you will do if your children tell your partner of your plan or if your partner otherwise finds out about your plan.

- Keep weapons like guns and knives locked away and as inaccessible as possible.

- Make a habit of backing the car into the driveway and keeping it fueled. Keep the driver's door unlocked and others locked — for a quick escape.

- Try not to wear scarves or long jewelry that could be used to strangle you.

- Create several plausible reasons for leaving the house at different times of the day or night.

- Call a domestic violence hotline periodically to assess your options and get a supportive understanding ear.

Getting Ready to Leave

- Keep any evidence of physical abuse, such as pictures.

- Know where you can go to get help; tell someone what is happening to you.

- If you are injured, go to a doctor or an emergency room and report what happened to you. Ask that they document your visit.

- Plan with your children and identify a safe place for them, like a room with a lock or a friend's house where they can go for help. Reassure them that their job is to stay safe, not to protect you.

- Contact your local battered women's shelter and find out about laws and other resources available to you before you have to use them during a crisis.

- Keep a journal of all violent incidences, noting dates, events and threats made, if possible.

- Acquire job skills or take courses at a community college as you can.

- Try to set money aside or ask friends or family members to hold money for you.

General Guidelines for Leaving an Abusive Relationship

- You may request a police stand-by or escort while you leave.

- If you need to sneak away, be prepared.

- Make a plan for how and where you will escape.

- Plan for a quick escape.

- Put aside emergency money as you can.

- Hide an extra set of car keys.

- Pack an extra set of clothes for yourself and your children and store them at a trusted friend or neighbor's house. Try to avoid using the homes of next-door neighbors, close family members and mutual friends.

- Take with you important phone numbers of friends, relatives, doctors, schools, etc., as well as other important items, including:

  o Driver's license

  o Regularly needed medication

  o Credit cards or a list of credit cards you hold yourself or jointly

  o Pay stubs

  o Checkbooks and information about bank accounts and other assets

- If time is available, also take:

  o Citizenship documents (such as your passport, green card, etc.)

  o Titles, deeds and other property information

  o Medical records

  o Children's school and immunization records

  o Insurance information

  o Copy of marriage license, birth certificates, will and other legal documents

  o Verification of social security numbers

  o Welfare identification

  o Valued pictures, jewelry or personal possessions

You may also create a false trail. Call motels, real estate agencies and schools in a town at least six hours away from where you plan to relocate. Ask questions that require a call back to your house in order to leave phone numbers on record.

After Leaving the Abusive Relationship

If getting a restraining order and the offender is leaving:

- Change your locks and phone number.

- Change your work hours and route taken to work.

- Change the route taken to transport children to school.

- Keep a certified copy of your restraining order with you at all times.

- Inform friends, neighbors and employers that you have a restraining order in effect.

- Give copies of the restraining order to employers, neighbors and schools along with a picture of the offender.

- Call law enforcement to enforce the order.

If you leave:

- Consider renting a post office box or using the address of a friend for your mail.

- Be aware that addresses are on restraining orders and police reports.

- Be careful to whom you give your new address and phone number.

- Change your work hours, if possible.

- Alert school authorities of the situation.

- Consider changing your children's schools.

- Reschedule appointments that the offender is aware of.

- Use different stores and frequent different social spots.

- Alert neighbors and request that they call the police if they feel you may be in danger.

- Talk to trusted people about the violence.

- Replace wooden doors with steel or metal doors. Install security systems if possible.

- Install a motion sensitive lighting system.

- Tell people you work with about the situation and have your calls screened by one receptionist if possible.

- Tell people who take care of your children who can pick up your children. Explain your situation to them and provide them with a copy of the restraining order.

- Call the telephone company to request caller ID. Ask that your phone number be blocked so that if you call anyone, neither your partner nor anyone else will be able to get your new, unlisted phone number.

Please call the 24-hour National Domestic Violence Hotline at 1-800-799-SAFE (7233) or TTY 1-800-787-3224 to discuss your concerns and questions.

Helpful websites:

Provides links to several resources:

http://www.womenlawyers.com/domestic.htm

Recognizing abuse:

http://helpguide.org/mental/domestic_violence_abuse_types_signs_causes_effects.htm

http://www.ehow.com/how_5069816_recognize-abusive-relationship.html

http://www.ehow.com/how_10016943_adult-children-recognize-abusive-relationships.html

How to help a friend or family member:

http://www.thehotline.org/get-educated/how-can-i-help-a-friend-or-family-member-who-is-being-abused/

How to get out of the abuse cycle:

http://www.livestrong.com/article/139559-steps-get-out-abusive-relationship/

http://www.ehow.com/how_2300751_prepare-flee-violent-relationship.html

Understanding the abuser:

http://tearsandhealing.com/abuse2.htm?&utm_content=ishe-notcrazy-UnstDis-StopAb&gclid=COONkvT-0asCFR5CgwodNmBnWg

Comments: hannavanora@gmail.com

www.ingramcontent.com/pod-product-compliance
Lightning Source LLC
Chambersburg PA
CBHW020241290526
45784CB00003B/1071